WINNER'S GUIDE TO
TEXAS
HOLD'EM
POKER

To my son Neil A. Warren, for your help and inspiration during the writing of this book.

To Bobbie Lea Stember, poker dealer at the Palace Station Casino in Las Vegas, for being such a shrewd judge of character. You had no idea how right you were when you told me after reading my notes for this book what a sick mind I had.

To Janet S. Thomson, poker player extraordinaire on the Mississippi Gulf Coast. Thank you for your support and help with proofreading and editing.

And to all of you who asked during my years of taking notes at the poker table, "You writing a book or something?" Here's your answer.

ABOUT THE AUTHOR

Ken Warren has entirely supported himself playing professional hold'em since he left the Air Force in 1987. An excellent tournament player, several Las Vegas poker rooms have asked Warren to skip their tournaments in order to give other players a chance to win as well. He is the auther of four other books and makes his home in Ocean Springs, Mississippi.

Ken Warren is the best of the new breed of riverboat poker players, and in fact, has the unique distinction of playing in and winning the very first legal poker hand dealt in Mississippi in this century. That landmark hand was kings full of sevens in the big blind position.

WINNER'S GUIDE TO
TEXAS HOLD'EM POKER

KEN WARREN

CARDOZA PUBLISHING

Cardoza Publishing is the foremost gaming and gambling publisher in the world with a library of more than 200 up-to-date and easy-to-read books and strategies. These authoritative works are written by the top experts in their fields and with more than 10,000,000 books in print, represent the best-selling and most popular gaming books anywhere.

See Page 256 for free book offer!!!

Copyright © 1996, 2000, 2008 by Ken Warren

Library of Congress Catalog Number: 2008927152
ISBN: 1-58042-230-6

TABLE OF CONTENTS

7. PRACTICAL WINNING HOLD'EM CONCEPTS 61

8. THE STRATEGY AND TACTICS OF HOLD'EM 111

1

INTRODUCTION

This book is *everything* that I wish someone had told me when I was first learning to play Texas hold'em. I will tell you how to play every hand, figure out whether to check, bet, raise, check-raise and fold, and how to handle any common situation that you'll face in this game. You'll understand the science of tells and the odds and mathematics involved in this game.

This book was written *by* a player *for* a player. One thing I am not, is a world champion poker player. What I am, is a successful low-limit hold'em player who has the ability to teach you what you need to know to win at Texas hold'em. And hopefully, I can do it in a manner that you'll find entertaining and easily readable.

This book is filled with many examples and illustrations of how to play specific hands in specific situations. I will give you practical advice about how to play every hold'em hand that you'll play for the rest of your poker-playing life. This book is a practical, hands-on guide to low-limit Texas hold'em that will help *you*, the average low-limit player. You'll see plenty of useful, practical advice on how to play Texas hold'em that you can't find collectively in any other poker book, or books, in the world.

The way I see it, there are only a handful of high stakes, world champion caliber poker players in the world. This book is meant for the other 150 million poker players who also want to be winners.

2

WHY PLAY TEXAS HOLD'EM?

Why play Texas hold'em? Because it's exciting, that's why. No other poker game is as exciting, intriguing, thrilling, fast, pot-building and as easy to learn as hold'em. Every day, especially with legalized gambling and poker playing in more and more states, more players are learning casino-style Texas hold'em. Seven-card stud players who try hold'em become instant converts. Texas hold'em has almost totally replaced seven-card stud in popularity in public poker rooms. And it's no wonder, when you consider the advantages that Texas hold'em has over seven-card stud:

IT'S A FASTER GAME
It's a much faster game. Instead of playing twenty hands per hour of stud, you can play up to forty hands per hour of hold'em. That's 100 percent more hands per hour; 100 percent more opportunities for the winning poker player (that's you) to win; 100 percent more opportunities for losing poker players (your opponents) to make more mistakes and 100 percent more money you can win.

THERE ARE NO EXPOSED CARDS
There are no exposed cards in the other player's hands for you to remember, as there are in seven-card stud, and

no cards that are exposed early in the hand and then folded that you'll have to remember. The only exposed cards in the game are the community cards and they stay exposed for all players to see throughout the hand.

NO EXCHANGING OF CARDS

There is no drawing or exchanging of cards as there is in five-card draw. You don't have to expend your mental energy trying to remember how many cards your opponents drew and trying to figure out what a zero-, one-, two- or three-card draw means. You and all the other players receive two cards at the beginning of the deal and you keep them until you either fold or there is a showdown at the end of the hand.

BETTING POSITION

You will be in the same betting position throughout each hand. The betting does not move around as it does in seven-card stud. There will be four betting rounds each hand. If you are first to bet at the beginning of the hand, you will bet first on each subsequent round of that hand. More importantly, if you're last to bet, you'll be last for all four rounds of betting (excluding the first betting round). Going last is an important strategic advantage and it's guaranteed to be yours throughout the hand.

THE POTS ARE BIGGER IN HOLD'EM

The pots are much bigger in hold'em than they are in stud or draw. Because hold'em is usually played ten- or even eleven-handed, there are more players to call the first rounds of betting to see the flop. Because there are more players in the hand, players who have straight or flush draws are getting the correct odds to attempt to make their hands. A player holding A♥ J♥ who gets a flop of 9♥ 6♥ 2♦ will always stay to the last card needing just one more heart. And if he hits his flush, he'll likely win a huge pot because as many as a half-dozen players will have put money in the pot on all four betting rounds.

YOU WIN MORE MONEY IN HOLD'EM

When you make a big hand in hold'em you usually win more of the other player's money than you would with the same hand in stud. If you make a full house in stud and rake in a $20 pot, you might have played against only one player, which means that up to half of that $20 was yours to begin with. You've won only $10. But if you make the same hand in a hold'em game, you likely would have beat six players, won a $100 pot, of which only $20 was yours to begin with. This phenomenon is attributed to the key unique feature of hold'em which is...

HOLD'EM HANDS ARE MORE COMPETITIVE

The final strength of all the player's hands will be closer in value than they are in stud or draw. In seven-card stud, seven players could play all the way to the end with seven different hands ranging in strength from no pair to a straight flush. Players with full houses will be competing for the pot against hands like one or two pair. And we all know that's no contest.

You don't have this situation in hold'em. Like stud, a hold'em hand consists of five of the best seven cards available to you. But unlike stud, five of the cards you can use to make up your hand also belong to every other player in the game. When 71 percent of your hand is the same as everyone else's hand, everybody is going to be in the running.

It is this community card concept that is the key, unique feature of hold'em. This is what brings the final strength of all the hands closer together and makes the game more competitive. When up to ten players can play one hand of poker at the same time, and 5/7ths of all of the hands are the same, it's a real contest.

And then there's one of the best features of all: You always get to see your opponent's last card. Since the river (last) card is always dealt face-up, you'll always know if a player could have completed a possible straight or flush draw.

YOU KNOW WHAT IT TAKES TO WIN

Before the flop, a pair of aces in the pocket is the best possible starting hand and if the game were over right there, you'd win every time with these cards. After that, though, the strength and value of your two pocket cards are determined by the community cards on the board. It is the cards on the board that determine what the best hand can be. Consider the following examples of boards and their best possible hands:

1. Q♦ 10♣ 7♥ 5♠ 2♣   Three queens

2. K♣ J♦ 9♥ 6♥ 3♦   Straight

3. Q♠ 9♥ 8♠ 7♣ 2♠   Flush

4. A♥ K♠ 5♣ 4♥ A♦   Full house or four of a kind

With the board paired, the best possible hand can be either a full house or four of a kind, depending on if you can account for one of the key cards. In the fourth example, a player can be holding A♣ A♠ to make four aces. If you are holding a single ace, then no one can have both aces to make four aces and therefore the best hand can only be a full house. A♣ K♦, A♠ 5♥ and A♠ 4♣ all make full houses. Notice though, that if you hold A♠ 4♣ (full house), another player can hold the A♣ with a 5 or a king to make a higher full house.

5. 10♦ 9♦ 7♦ 5♠ 3♥   Straight flush

6. K♣ Q♣ 10♣ 9♠ 6♠   Royal flush

IT'S EASIER TO FOLD IN HOLD'EM

If you're drawing to a straight or flush in hold'em and you miss, it's pretty much automatic that you can throw your hand away without having to call on the end. If you made a pair while trying to make your flush, you might be tempted to call on the end in a stud game. In a hold'em game, that pair is not as good a hand when that flush card does not come on the end.

YOU KNOW WHEN TO PLAY OR NOT PLAY AFTER THE FIRST ROUND OF BETTING

In hold'em you're a big favorite to win the hand if you started out with the best hand. Because of the community cards, it's just too difficult for a single opponent to outdraw you. This is especially true as the hand progresses and players drop out along the way. But that's not true in stud, where you can start with the best hand and easily be outrun by almost any other hand.

Here's the essence of Texas hold'em: The object of the game is to have either the best hand or a draw to the best hand after the flop. You should fold just about all other hands after the flop. You are just too big an underdog to continue playing and the reason you know that is that you can compare your pocket cards to the flop. You can't do that in stud because you can see only one of your opponent's first three cards. You often have to invest more money in a stud hand before you realize you have to fold.

THE JACKPOTS ARE BIGGER IN HOLD'EM

If you play poker in a casino you'll find that there is often a **bad beat jackpot**. This is a pool of money that is collected by taking a small amount from every pot that reaches a certain amount, usually $20. This money is set aside and is awarded in part to the player who makes an incredibly good hand, usually aces full, and gets it beat by an even better hand, usually four of a kind. Because hold'em is a faster game, more hands are played per hour than in stud, and the minimum pot size required to rake the pot for the jackpot is reached more often. When you do hit a jackpot, it will usually be bigger than if you were in a stud game and it is usually hit in less playing time than in a stud game.

3

HOW TO BEAT TEXAS HOLD'EM

BETTING LIMITS

Texas hold'em is played for a wide variety of limits. What all of these limits have in common is that they adhere to the same betting structure, which is a 1 to 2 ratio. The bets before the flop and on the flop will be exactly one small bet, the lower betting tier, and the bets on the turn and the river will be exactly one big bet, the higher betting tier (twice the small bet).

The most common betting limits are $1/$2, $2/$4, $3/$6, $4/$8, $5/$10, $10/$20, $15/$30, $20/$40, $30/$60, $60/$120, $100/$200 and $300/$600. You must bet exactly the amount mentioned and that is why this is called a structured game. You cannot bet $4 or $5 in a $3/$6 game.

Another betting structure that has become very popular is called $1-$4-$8-$8 limit. This means that you may bet from $1 to $4 before the flop, and you may bet from $1 to $4 after the flop. On the turn you can bet between $1 and $8 and you can make the same bet on the river.

NUMBER OF PLAYERS

Texas hold'em can be played with as few as two players and with as many as twenty-two players. The most desirable number of players is ten and many Las Vegas poker rooms seat exactly that number.

HIGH HAND WINS

Hold'em is played for high only; standard high hand wins. There are no wild cards. Remember, the final poker hand is made up of exactly five cards.

SMALL BLIND AND BIG BLIND

The blinds are used to force action from the first two players to the left of the dealer by having them put money into the pot before the cards are dealt. The big blind is always the same as the small bet and the small blind is one-half of the big blind. For example in a $2/$4 game, the player to the immediate left of the dealer puts $1 into the pot, called the **small blind**. The player to the left of the small blind puts $2 into the pot, called the **large**, or **big blind**. (The one exception to this blind structure is when the game is short-handed, and then there is only the big blind. This will be covered in detail in a later chapter.)

Due to the fact that there are two blinds, there is no ante in Texas hold'em cash games as there is in stud and draw poker. In tournaments, an ante is usually added after the third round of play.

PLAY OF THE GAME
Initial Two Cards

Each player is dealt two cards face down. These cards are called the **pocket cards**. Do not show these cards to any other player since this constitutes your entire private hand.

Starting with the player to the immediate left of the big blind, and moving clockwise, each player has the option of either **folding**, (opting out of play by **mucking**—getting rid of—your cards), **calling** (keeping your hand and putting the correct amount of money in the pot), or **raising**, increasing the bet by an amount at least as much as the previous bet.

If no one has raised by the time the action comes back to the small blind, he can either fold, call the remainder of the big blind bet, or raise at least the amount of the big blind. For example, in a $1-$4-$8-$8 game, a raise of $1 is not allowed because all raises in poker must be for at least the amount of the previous bet. In a structured game ($3/$6 or $5/$10), the raise must be the small-tiered amount. Since the blinds had to put their money in the pot before they saw their hands, they have the option of raising themselves.

If no one has raised by the time the action gets back to the big blind, he then has an option to raise. The dealer will ask him, "Option?" and the big blind has to answer with either, "Check" ("I bet nothing"), or "I raise." The raise is the same as the lower tier bet.

The Flop

After the first betting round, the dealer **burns** the top card, removes it from play, and turns the next three cards face up on the board. This is the **flop**. There is a round of betting with a small bet and a three-raise limit. Players may **check**, not bet but still stay active, and pass play on to the next player until someone bets. However, once a bet is made, the player must either call the bet or raise, or he must fold and go out of play. Checking is no longer possible once a bet is made. This is true on this and all future rounds. Some casinos have a four-raise or even a five-raise limit, so it is wise to ask before you start playing.

The Turn

After all the betting on the flop is complete, the top card of the deck will be burned. This assumes, of course, that two or more players remain to compete for the pot. Then a fourth card, called the **turn** card, is placed face up on the table. A round of betting follows, only this time you can bet from $1 to $8 in a $1-$4-$8-$8 game, or the higher tier in a structured game. For example, in a $3/$6 game, you now must bet or raise in $6 increments.

The River

After the turn betting is completed, the top card is again burned, and a fifth, and final, card will be turned face up on the table. This is called the **river** or **end**. There is a final round of betting according to the same betting guidelines as on the turn.

The Showdown

After all the action is complete, there is a **showdown**. All the active players who want to claim the pot then show their hands. Using his two pocket cards and the five cards on the board, the dealer then determines what the best poker hand is, and awards the pot to that player. High hand wins.

The dealer button then moves one player to the left, marking the new dealer's position. The two mandatory blinds will be posted before the next round of cards are dealt.

Note that in all variations of poker, any time that one player is left, because all the other players have folded, the last remaining player automatically wins the pot by default.

RANKS OF POKER HANDS AND WHY THEY'RE RANKED THAT WAY

The ranks of poker hands are standardized today, but it wasn't always like that. Gone are the days when a poker player could make a *skip*, *blaze*, *tiger* or any number of other exotic poker hands. Poker hands are ranked the way they are today based on one cold, hard fact: the exact odds of being dealt that hand in exactly five cards. The more difficult it is to receive a certain five-card hand, the higher it's ranked on the scale of poker hands.

One important point to make here is that a poker hand is determined by using only five cards, regardless of how many you're dealt, how many cards you have to choose from or exactly which style or game of poker you're playing. Also, there is no such thing as any one suit taking precedence over another suit as in some bidding or trump card games. A royal flush in hearts is no higher or lower a poker hand than a royal flush in spades.

Remember to use all the cards on the board in hold'em, especially when you make two pair. If you have A♥ 6♥ and the board is A♣ J♦ J♥ 10♠ 4♦, you're not beat just because your opponent has A♠ 9♠. You both have aces and jacks with a 10 kicker.

POKER HAND RANKINGS

The following poker hands are listed in order of strength from highest in rank to lowest in rank.

Royal Flush: A-K-Q-J-10 of the same suit. There are only four royal flushes possible, one for each suit.

Straight Flush: A hand that has five cards of the same suit in sequence.

Four of a Kind: Four cards of the same rank. The fifth card is irrelevant unless, in hold'em, the community cards show the four of a kind.

Full House: Three of a kind and one pair. The three of a kind determines the highest full house in the event there is more than one full house in a hand.

Flush: Five cards of the same suit that do not make a straight flush.

Straight: Five cards in sequence but not of the same suit.

Three of a Kind: Three cards of the same rank.

Two Pair: Two different pairs with one odd card.

One Pair: One pair with three odd cards.

High Card: Five cards that cannot make any one of the above hands. In this case, the hand with the highest-ranking card is the winner. A-9-5-4-3 beats K-Q-9-5-4.

There are 2,598,960 ways to be dealt one particular poker hand in five cards. The following chart shows how it breaks down into all possible poker hands.

Odds of Being Dealt Poker Hands

Poker Hand	Odds Against	Example
Royal Flush	649,739 to 1	A♦ K♦ Q♦ J♦ 10♦
Straight Flush	64,973 to 1	7♣ 6♣ 5♣ 4♣ 3♣
Four of a Kind	4,164 to 1	8♠ 8♥ 8♦ 8♣ Q♠
Full House	693 to 1	K♣ K♦ K♥ 10♠ 10♥
Flush	508 to 1	A♥ J♥ 9♥ 7♥ 3♥
Straight	254 to 1	Q♠ J♥ 10♦ 9♣ 8♠
Three of a Kind	46 to 1	7♥ 7♦ 7♣ K♥ 2♦
Two Pair	20 to 1	J♣ J♦ 5♥ 5♠ 9♠
One Pair	1.25 to 1	9♥ 9♦ A♥ 8♠ 2♦
No Pair	1.002 to 1.000	A♥ T♠ 9♦ 5♣ 2♠

The only poker game that these odds apply to directly is five-card stud, a game where you're dealt exactly five cards with no opportunity to draw or otherwise exchange your cards. The exact odds of being dealt the above hands in seven-card stud and Texas hold'em will vary of course, because you'll have seven cards with which to make your best five card hand. But that doesn't change the fact that the above list is the agreed-upon convention, and it applies to all forms of poker.

MISTAKES AND DISPUTES

Any time you have a poker dealer dealing hands to players at the rate of 40 hands per hour, there are bound to be a few mistakes. Some of the more common errors are burning and dealing the turn or river card before the action from the previous betting round is complete, accidentally exposing one of the blind's first cards, miscalling hands on the river, and pushing the pot to the wrong player.

Sometimes you'll look down and see A♣ A♥, K♥ K♠ or A♦ K♠ and then hear the dealer say, "Bring 'em back," because of a misdeal. Keep in mind that those cards were never really yours to begin with because you would not have gotten them if the dealer had dealt the hand correctly.

Mistakes and disputes are an integral part of the game of poker and you should stay calm and take it all in stride.

ALL IN

Sometimes a player will be involved in a hand and run out of money to bet before the hand is over. Since all casino poker games are *table stakes* only, you are not allowed to put more money on the table in the middle of a hand. When you run out of money and put your last dollar in the pot, you are said to be **all in** and you cannot win any more money than what is in the pot at this point (that is, once other players match your last bet or raise).

As an example, lets say you have Q♦ J♥ in the pocket, and you have $14 in chips (called **checks** in a casino poker game) in front of you at the beginning of the hand. From the small blind, you call $2 to see the flop along with two other players. The flop is 10♣ 9♦ 4♥, you bet $4, and are called by the same two players. There is now $18 in the pot. The turn is the 6♠ and you check and call with your last $8. Two opponents have also put in $8, so there is now $42 in the pot, but you are now out of money. That $42 pot is all you can win.

The dealer puts that pot aside and all future betting goes into a **side pot** that you cannot win any part of, since you cannot put money into it. The river card is the K♣, making you the nut straight. One of the other players in the hand bets $8 and is called by the other player, creating a side pot with $16 in it. The dealer asks to see only the two hands involved in the side pot (hold on to your cards and don't show them to the dealer until asked), and awards the side pot to the player who has the best of the two hands.

The dealer then asks to see your hand to determine if you can beat the winner of the side pot. Since you have the best hand you are awarded the main pot of $42. In effect, you got to play the river card for free (you don't have to fold when you're all in), but you couldn't win the side pot even though you made the best hand.

4

HISTORY OF POKER AND A LITTLE TRIVIA

- Many early Oriental playing cards were actually sticks that were later widened and shortened and designed with images.

- Playing cards were most likely invented in China in 1120 A.D.

- Playing cards were introduced into Europe in the 1300s.

- When Columbus landed in North America in 1492, his men plucked wide leaves from trees, drew images on them and played cards.

- Due to French influence, spades represents nobility, diamonds represents merchants, clubs represents the peasants and hearts represents the clergy.

- Edmond Hoyle lived to be 97 years old but he still died 150 years before poker was invented or played in America.

- Hoyle's book, *A Short Treatise on the Game of Whist*, was about bridge, not poker.

- In the 1800s, 2,000 to 2,500 riverboat gamblers played poker on America's waterways. By contemporary accounts, no more than four of these poker players were honest all the time. A straight beat a flush at this time.

- Historians generally agree that Wild Bill Hickock was a lousy poker player.

- Dead Man's Hand is two pair, aces and eights, the cards Wild Bill Hickok was holding when he was shot. Contrary to popular belief, the exact suits or colors (black or red) he was holding when he was shot in the back is just not known today.

- Jack McCall killed Wild Bill Hickok because he thought he had been cheated out of a twenty-five cent pot (he probably had been). That's equal to $32.15 in 2008 dollars.

- Groucho Marx got his name from carrying his poker money in a "grouch bag."

- A fifth suit of cards, called Eagle, was introduced in 1937 but never caught on. The reason for it was to force the public to buy new decks of cards.

- Former President Richard Nixon won $6,000 playing poker in his first two months in the U.S. Navy during WWII. That's equal to $54,607 in 2008 dollars. He used that money, and more poker winnings, to finance his run for the U.S. Congress in 1946, which he won.

- Returning from the Potsdam Conference in 1945, President Harry S. Truman played pot-limit poker sixteen hours a day for a week with the press corps.

- At least 65,000,000 Americans regularly play poker.

- Las Vegas casinos are not legally obligated to pay off their gambling debts.

5

CASINO HOLD'EM ADVICE

13 POKER ROOM TIPS

Here is some good advice that applies before you play your first hand of hold'em in a casino poker room:

1. What's a Low-Limit Game?

Keep in mind that what makes a low-limit game is the skill level of the players themselves, not just the limit that is being played. If you walk into a poker room and you see ten high-limit players playing in the smallest game in the house, then this is not a true low-limit game and you should avoid it like the plague. You will often see this situation when there is a list for a high-limit game, but there aren't enough players to actually start the game. So these players will sit in a low-limit game while they're waiting for their game to get started.

On the other hand, if you see ten of the worst players you know playing in a $10/$20 game, you'll know that that's not a true high-limit game either.

It's the skill level of the players that determines the true characteristics of a game. Keep this in mind if you have your choice of more than one low-limit game to get into.

2. What Limit to Play?

If you've never played before, or if you have very little experience at hold'em, you should play in the lowest limit game you can find. There are some excellent $2/$4 games out there, but I recommend you move to a higher limit as soon as you're able to. The specific advice contained in this book is geared for that limit and this structure has big advantages for the serious player that will be explained later in this book.

3. Phone Numbers

If you play often, carry a list of the phone numbers of the poker rooms you frequent most and call ahead to get on the list of players waiting to get into a game. That way you can move up the list while you're on the way to the cardroom.

4. Getting There

If possible, go by yourself and have your own transportation. Nothing screws up a good poker game like having your spouse or friend pull you out of the game because he or she had to go or they have the only means of transportation.

5. Supplies

Before you leave the house, make sure you have the following items with you. If necessary buy yourself one of those hip hugger pouches that you wear with the strap around your waist.

• A sweater or jacket. Even if it's 110 degrees outside you may be sitting still for hours at a poker table situated right under an air conditioner vent. It can get very, very cold.

• Prescription glasses if you have them. Even if you don't ordinarily wear them, you'll find that after ten hours of squinting at cards in a dimly lit, possibly smoke-filled poker room, your eyes could use a rest. It's especially helpful if you have prescription sunglasses. You'll often be in a seat where the glare of the lights hits the cards just right and you won't be able to see anything. At its worst, it looks like a small mirror in the middle of the table aimed right at your eyes. Good, polarized, lightweight sunglasses are a blessing.

• Bring aspirin, Tylenol®, ibuprofin, antacid, and all the cigarettes and medicine you use regularly. Many casinos have a policy against providing aspirin for gamblers—something about liability insurance. Cigarettes bought from a casino bar can cost as much as $4 per pack.

> **Hot Tip**
> If you do run out of cigarettes while you're playing and you feel that it will affect your play, then I strongly recommend that you go ahead and pay whatever it takes to get a cigarette between your lips again. Four dollars for a pack of cigarettes is a small price to pay compared to what you could lose playing poker while fretting over a cigarette.

6. Time Limit

If possible, have an open-ended time limit on your play. Game conditions change and you should play as long as you're a favorite to win in the game. I recommend that you don't play if you know you can play for only a few minutes.

Also, don't play for any length of time if you feel like you wouldn't feel well enough to sit through a two-hour movie. If you don't feel well enough to watch a movie then you certainly don't feel well enough to play strongly in a poker game.

7. Scope Out the Game

If you have to wait for a seat you should watch the game you intend to play in. If possible, talk to a friend in the game to get a briefing regarding the opposition and who is using what style of play. Find out who the real beginners are, if there are any.

Also, listen to the table talk. Too many low-limit players will talk about the hand they just passed, what their last hand was, why they played it the way they did, or why they didn't play the hand. These players will put you on the inside track to their thought process without making you learn the hard way.

8. Keep Learning

If you can't watch the game you're going to be in, then utilize your waiting time by reading the latest issue of *Card Player* magazine if there are any poker magazines available. Your poker education should be an ongoing, lifetime endeavor. You have to work at it just like you would any other serious job.

9. Watch for Beginners

Pay attention to the floor personnel and the dealers because you might see them explain how to play the game to a customer. When you see this player in the game, you'll know he's a beginner. Two good clues that you're playing against a beginner is when you hear a player asking a lot of questions about how to play the game and when a player keeps his poker chips in a rack to play out of. It slows up the game terribly. The more experienced players don't do that.

10. House Rules

The house rules should be posted conspicuously nearby. Read them. Typical house rules look something like this:

- All games are table stakes. No short buy-ins (or one) are permitted.

- Only one player per hand.
- Check and raise is allowed.
- One bet and three raises maximum, unless heads-up.
- No string bets allowed.
- Players are responsible for protecting their own hand.
- No food/reading at the table.
- Any player at the table may ask to see any called hand at the end.*
- The decision of the floor person is final.

11. Jackpot Games

Find out if there's a jackpot in the game you're going to get into. Depending on the limit, there may or may not be one. It's possible that even though a jackpot is advertised in the cardroom, you may be in a game that doesn't have one. Ask.

12. How Many Hands?

Notice if the game you're going to be in is nine- or ten-handed. Sometimes a player will leave the game without the floorperson noticing and the game will go on nine-handed without anyone realizing it. A game is not necessarily full just because the floorperson thinks it's already full.

13. Comps Available

Find out if the poker room offers any type of comps to the poker players. Most of them do. The typical deal is that the poker room will treat you to a free meal in the casino restaurant if you play poker for a minimum amount of time. You can usually still get the comp if you lose all of your money before you've played the minimum three hours or so. Most poker rooms keep track of your hours by having you swipe your player's club card.

*At the showdown, any player at the table can ask to see any called hand, regardless of whether he's in the pot or not. If the hand is not called, no one may ask to see the hand.

17 GAME-PLAYING TIPS

Systematically reviewing the above list will pretty much prepare you to play hold'em without encountering some of the most common problems that face beginners. The floorman has just called your name and you've just been seated in a Texas hold'em game. Here's what you should keep in mind now that action is coming your way:

1. How Much Should You Buy in For?

Absolutely no less than $100 in a $1-$4-$8-$8 game, proportionately more in higher limits. You need to have enough money in the game to play your hands correctly without regard to how many chips you have in front of you at any one time. You must be able to lose a hand and still have enough chips left to put a lot of bets in the next pot if the hand calls for it.

If you've decided that you'll put $20 or $40 more into the game should you lose some of your original $100 buy-in, then you should go ahead and buy in for the whole $120 or $140 in the beginning. If you lose $40 of a $100 buy-in, that would represent a 40 percent loss to you. But a $40 loss with a $140 buy-in is only a 28 percent loss to you. Psychologically, you'll feel better about it and you'll still have more money left in your stack.

If you've decided that you're going to rebuy should the need arise, then you should rebuy *at that time* for the largest additional amount that you're willing to put into the game. Don't wait to rebuy once you've made the decision. Do not put $20 on the table and lose that, then put $20 more out, and lose that, and so on. When you do that, you're playing your money and not your cards. That's a sure prescription for disaster.

2. New Player

In most low-limit games, a new player does not have to play his first hand in the big blind. You have the option of not playing for two hands and when the deal passes your position, you can receive a hand just to the right of the dealer. This means you can look at eight hands for free before you have to put in your $2 big blind.

3. Which Hand to Miss

If you have to miss one hand for any reason, the best hand to miss is when you're just to the left of the big blind. Because of your position relative to the other players, this is when you're at the biggest positional disadvantage of any player at the table. The playing requirements are so high for this position that you'll almost never have missed a good, playable hand. There'll be more about this later when we talk about what hands to play in which positions.

4. When to Take a Break

If you have to be away from the table long enough to miss two hands, then the best time is when it is your big blind. Get up and do not play when it is your big blind or small blind. Then, after the dealer button passes your position, put in both your big and small blinds (you must make up missed blinds in this game). You will be coming back into the game in the best of all possible positions, late position, and you will have already called to see the flop.

5. Don't Lose Your Seat

Remember that if you leave the game for more than one hour in most cardrooms, you are subject to having your checks picked up (though held for you) and your seat given to another player.

6. Pick a Good First Hand

As obvious as it may sound, choose the first hand you voluntarily enter the pot with very carefully. It really helps when you can win your first hand. It will give you extra room to play future hands more freely. On the other hand, when you lose your first hand, you'll have to start out by trying to dig yourself out of a hole and that affects your attitude toward the game.

7. Don't Drink Alcohol

Do not drink even one alcoholic beverage, unless you're not going to play poker after your drink. The advantage that you have as a poker player over the other patrons in the casino is that your decisions matter. When you play poker, you're not playing against the house. You're playing against other poker players. And the fact is that, in the long run, good players beat bad players.

When you drink, you give away your edge as a good player and you become no better, and often worse, than the bad players. If you must drink, buy something with your poker winnings at the liquor store on the way home after the game.

8. Don't Splash the Pot

That means you should put your bets in a neat stack directly in front of you so that all concerned can see how much you're betting and the dealer can move the game along faster. When you throw your checks into the pot no one can be sure exactly how much you bet. It's for the protection of all. There are players who deliberately throw six checks into the pot and then say, "I bet $8."

9. Let the Dealer Make the Change

If you call a $2 bet with a $5 check, let the dealer give you the $3 change. It may be raised $4 more behind you and it saves time to just say, "$1 more, please," since you already have $5 out there. Hold'em is pretty much an automatic game as far as decision-making is concerned, and every little thing that speeds up the game is appreciated by all.

10. Be Ready to Act When it's Your Turn

You'll instantly know what you want to do 95 percent of the time and you'll often know what you intend to do even before it's your turn to act. When it is your turn to act, say what it is you intend to do. A verbal declaration of your intent made in turn is binding upon you. This will allow the players behind you to think and start to act on their hands while you're putting chips in the pot or folding your hand.

11. Don't Act Out of Turn

It's very time consuming to reconstruct the action and correct sequence of events after someone has acted out of turn. This also means that you should not make distracting remarks about your hand or your intent to call or raise out of turn. Good players do not have to rely on tricks or ruses of this type to win at poker.

12. Don't "Hollywood"

Don't needlessly delay on purpose when it is your turn to act. While there is no rule against it, it is considered rude in poker to take an inordinately long time to make a play that you knew you were going to make from the beginning anyway. The benefit of this is that on those rare occasions when you do need extra time to figure out what to do, the dealer and the other players will gladly give you all the time you need.

13. Don't Criticize

You shouldn't make comments that could be construed as criticism, or to actually criticize another player's play— even when he hits a 1,080 to 1 longshot to beat your full house (it's happened to me). There is no need to needle losers or make fun of winners who are playing badly. And besides, you can be asked to leave the game for criticizing another player's play. Even a dealer who makes a comment about your play can be fired for it.

14. Don't Get Involved in Other Players' Disputes

If there is a dispute or if there is an irregularity in the play of a hand, you should not say anything unless you are involved in the pot. The dealer, the participants in the pot, and the floorperson will straighten it out. It's been my experience that you only make things worse if you try to get involved in a dispute that is not yours.

15. Rake Break

When the game gets short-handed, ask the house for a *rake break*. The house can reduce the rake to as low as $1 per hand or even let you play with no rake, but there is one rule you have to know about: The dealers are not allowed to suggest it first since they work for the house and the rake is how the house makes their money. Asking for a $1 rake and a $1 jackpot drop is known as a "Code 11."

Also, be aware that if you play with a reduced rake, you may not eligible to win the jackpot if there is one. If you have a choice of playing with a full rake and a jackpot, or a reduced rake and no jackpot, you should always opt for the reduced rake and no jackpot. That's the way to make the most money in the long run, according to the odds.

16. Switching Seats

If you happen to be in a seat that you're not happy with, you should be on the lookout for other players about to vacate their seats. The first player to inform the dealer that he desires a certain seat is first in line for that seat. There will be more about why you should change seats later in this book.

17. I Saved the Most Important Tip for Last

When you win a hand, don't give your cards to the dealer until the dealer pushes the pot to you.

TIPPING ADVICE

How much should you tip a dealer when you win a hand? If you already play in a casino, you already have an idea of what is comfortable for you. I personally tip a dealer fifty cents for pots up to $50 and $1 for pots over $50. The dealer is not your partner in this game, he does not risk any money like you do, and he certainly does not give you any money when you lose a hand. The dealer doesn't share any of the risk you take when you put your money in the pot.

I believe that the dealers are not automatically entitled to a percentage of your wins and you therefore do not have to tip more just because you win more. I do, however, believe in tipping for good, efficient, friendly, competent service. If you play poker regularly, you will find that dealer tokes can be a significant part of your win if you let them get out of hand. You should look at poker playing as your business, and tips as part of the overhead.

ONE MORE TIP

Here's one miscellaneous thought to wrap up this chapter and get you in the right frame of mind to study and enjoy the rest of this book: Motivation times Ability equals Performance (M x A = P). If your motivation is high and your ability is high, then your performance will be high. If your performance is low, then you will have to determine if either your motivation or ability (or both) is low. I will leave this up to you to figure out how this applies to poker.

6

WINNING POKER CONCEPTS

This chapter gives you advice that applies equally well to all forms of poker. This advice covers most of the games you would play in a home game and any hold'em game in any casino in the country. After this chapter we will advance to specific practical advice that applies only to hold'em.

GET READY TO PLAY

You have to be in the right frame of mind to play poker. It is, after all, a game of skill. You have to use your brain. So it figures that the condition of your brain should be of concern to you. Ideally, you should be fresh, well rested, free of mental distractions and problems, and have the desire and ability to play. You should have uppermost in your mind exactly what the object of poker is (to make money) and exactly how to go about it.

Here are some specific tips to help you get ready to play:

The Object of This Game is to Make Money

Unless you're playing with the kids for matchsticks or have to lose to the boss for job security reasons, you should look at your poker playing buddies as miniature walking, talking gold mines.

If you keep records of your poker sessions, and you will if you read this book, you'll see that your poker playing time is worth so much per hour to you. It's just like working for someone else for a wage. How much you make per hour is up to you, your skill and the games you choose to play in.

Be Prepared to Beat Any Poker Game

How much you like or dislike a particular poker game should have nothing to do with how profitable it can be for you. If you are to be a real poker player, you should be able to play any type of game you run into. The key to this attitude is the fact that you know that any type of poker game can be objectively analyzed and there is usually one best way to play.

Concentrate on Making the Correct Decisions

The object of poker is to make money, but how do you go about it? How do you win money from nine other people who are trying to win your money? There are several answers to this dilemma.

First of all, you are often playing with people who aren't trying to win your money. They play because they like to socialize, they like the excitement of the game and it's what they want to do with their time. Here's the most important tip I can give you about your opponents, especially in a casino game: A lot of the people you play against in a casino hold'em game are there not because they're poker players, but because they're gamblers and they have discovered that playing poker is how they can get the most bang for their buck.

Even though the object of poker is to make money, that's not what you should be thinking about during the game. The only thing that should matter to you is the quality of the decisions you make. When it is your turn to check, call, bet, raise or fold, you should make the best decision possible at the time with the information you have.

Poker is a game of skill, but the real skill is in the decision-making. Wouldn't you agree that a consistent winner at this game is a good decision maker? And wouldn't you agree that the guy who loses the most money in your game makes the worst decisions?

Whoever makes the best decisions in the long run, will win the most money in the long run. Your job in this game is to consistently make the best decisions you can when it is your turn to act, and not to worry about the money or even how the hand turns out. Don't even worry about winning the pot you're in. Once you make the correct decision, it doesn't matter what happens after that.

> Whoever makes the best decisions in the long run will win the most money in the long run.

It is possible to do the right thing and still lose the hand, but you won't lose the game in the long run. You know it's possible to do the wrong thing and still win the hand but that doesn't mean that deliberately playing incorrectly is the way to play all the time. Play the best way you know how and the money will come.

Profit from Superior Decision-Making

Realize that your profit from this game comes from the mistakes your opponents make. If the quality of decision-making is equal among all the players, then there won't be many mistakes made and any one player's profit or loss will not be that much more or less than any others.

It's when one player (you) has the ability to make decisions that are superior to the opposition that you will make a lot of money in this game. You don't have to be an expert to be in this position. If you are a good player in a game full of poor players you should be able to clean up in the long run.

Don't Drink Alcohol When You Play, Not Even One Drink

If you play in a casino you'll see that all the alcohol you can drink is served to you free of charge right at the poker table.

As we spoke about before, since you play poker against other players and not against the house, they are not providing these drinks in an attempt to get you drunk and then take advantage of your drunken state by making you play badly. The real purpose of serving you free drinks in a casino is to make you want to stay and play longer. This exposes you to the house edge in whatever game you're playing and it affects your decisions. This is why a blackjack player who is ahead $600 will stay and play until it's all gone or why the slots player who hits a $300 jackpot will put it all back in the machine trying to hit an even bigger jackpot.

In a way, the slots player who is drinking has an advantage over you. His decisions don't matter. There is only one way to pull the lever on a slot machine but there are a hundred different ways to play a poker hand and they all require that you be able to make good decisions. Let the other players drink; you'll get their money that much faster.

Play Aggressively

You cannot check and call in hold'em and be a winner. There's a term that describes a weak, passive hold'em player, and it's a **calling station**. So many more good things can happen to you when you bet instead of check. If you are a calling station then you can win only by having the best hand at the showdown. You will never be able to take advantage of strategic moves like check-raising, semibluffing, bluffing and using deception in playing your hand.

You have a dozen ways to win a hand if you're a complete poker player, and having the best hand when your bet is called at the end is only one of them. You're giving up a lot of money and opportunities if the only thing you know how to do is to wait for the nuts.

Remember: It's One Long Poker Game

Look at your poker playing as one long poker game that lasts a lifetime but is interrupted by sleeping, eating, working and vacationing. The first hand that you play today is just the next hand after the last hand you played yesterday. You should take an even-tempered approach, and realize that whether you're winning or losing is determined by your overall Win/Loss record.

How you're doing today is not as important as your trend of wins or losses and your actual cumulative total.

It's critical that you keep records of your poker playing so that you know exactly where you stand. It will help you analyze your performance and detect trends in your play. You may realize that you consistently lose playing at one particular casino, you may lose on Wednesdays; you may lose when you play too many hours in one session, or other things.

There is an appendix at the back of this book that has a form that you can copy and use to record your wins and losses.

Know When to Leave the Game

Use whatever criteria that is important to you, but have some definite idea of when you should leave the game. You can set a time limit—leave when you've won or lost a certain amount of money or you can do what I do: leave when you're no longer a favorite to win money in the game. There are a variety of reasons why you'd no longer be a favorite in a particular game:

   a. You're already losing and you don't see any chance of getting it back in this session.

b. You're tired or otherwise distracted.

c. Some of the bad players have left and they've been replaced by better players.

d. There's little or practically no money on the table even though there are players in the seats.

e. You have won so much money that there just isn't any left to win. My advice is to leave the game if you should have over half the money on the table. At this point, you are risking too much to win too little. It's difficult to win more than half of the money on the table and if you stay beyond that you'll often find that you'll be feeding money back to the other players.

f. You're being outplayed for some reason. You may be ill or mentally below par and not realize it. If the gang that you usually beat up is beating up on you, you should quit the game.

g. You started out with a few losing hands and now have discovered that when you have a winning hand, you don't get any action.

Choose Your Game Carefully

If you have your choice of more than one game to play in, try to play in the one that has the greatest number of players entering every pot. This means it is a loose game and it should be very profitable for you. Try to find a game with a lot of alcohol and lots of money on the table for the betting limit.

ANALYZING YOUR OPPONENTS

When you play poker, what you're really doing is matching your brainpower against the intellectual ability of your opponents in such a way that you always know how you measure up. How much you're winning or losing is how you keep score in this game. It is critical that you know as much as possible about your opponents. You, of course, can't know everything, but there is a lot that you can deduce on your own.

The number one fault of most low-limit players is that they will see the flop with hands they should have folded. They will also call when they should fold and play their hands long after it's clear they're beat or don't have the right odds to play. In short, they play too loose.

You will hardly ever see a beginning low-limit hold'em player play too conservatively or too tight. If a low-limit player has the option of either calling or folding, and it's an even toss-up what the correct play is, he will almost always decide to call. That's one reason why it's so difficult to bluff out a player on the end. Beginners come to play and it's no fun to fold without them calling one final bet to see what they have. Hearing players say, "Well, I came this far" and "He might be bluffing" are two sure signs of the typical low-limit player.

The major difference between low-limit and medium to high-limit players is that the latter do a lot more raising preflop and on the flop to protect their hands during the cheap betting rounds. If you're on a draw, they'll know it and they'll make you pay the maximum allowed by the house rules. Any hand from a pair on up is a favorite over a straight or a flush draw and if your draw is going to win, then you're just going to have to pay for the privilege.

If you find yourself in a game where there's an inordinate amount of raises on the flimsiest of cards, then that's a sure sign that you're playing against talent superior to yours and you should get out. You're no longer a favorite in the game.

If you don't know how a player plays, you should assume he plays well, or at least as well as you do until you have concrete evidence to the contrary. If you see him play a 7♥ 5♥ in early position, if he calls with second or third pair to the river, if he consistently calls on the end with a losing hand, and if the players on his right often successfully check-raise him. You can mark him down as a poor player.

There is, however, one popular method of detecting poor players that I think is overrated and not that reliable. It is the method of watching to see how many or what proportion of pots he voluntarily enters to see the flop. The conventional wisdom says that if he plays very few hands besides the blinds then he is a tight player and if he sees the flop with half of his hands then he is a loose player. This line of reasoning is probably better than no information at all but it can often lead you to the wrong conclusion.

There are 1,326 different possible two-card combinations that you can be dealt before the flop and if you discount similar hands (i.e., J♦ 2♦ is the same hand as J♠ 2♠), then there are only 169 different possible hands.

With that many different hands out there it is possible, and often likely, that you can't find a playable hand in the first 100 hands you're dealt. This means that when you see a player enter the game and not play a hand for three hours, it's not always because he actually is a tight player. In this case, you should evaluate the quality of his play based on the actual cards that you see him turn over at the ends of his hands.

It is possible to walk into a casino poker room and determine, just by observing the players, just who you would like to play against and who you wouldn't. Here is a list of players you would like to play against:

PLAYERS YOU WANT TO PLAY AGAINST

1. Off-duty Casino Employees

Skill at dealing poker does not equate to skill at playing poker. Dealing three hundred hands of poker a day does not teach you how to play poker. I've seen the magician levitate the girl 100 times, but I don't know how to do it. (And a sincere "thank you" to all you poker dealers who bought a copy of this book.)

2. Talkative, Loud, Smiling, Cheerful Players

If they're doing all that, they can't possibly be devoting enough mental energy to the game to beat the player who is concentrating on the game.

3. Players who Drink Alcohol

A player who's been drinking will start to play more carelessly, bet and call when he shouldn't, bluff when he shouldn't and generally play too many hands. And he'll usually stay and play and drink until he's broke.

4. Players Who Expose Cards

There are players who just aren't careful enough to protect their hands. If you meet one, I recommend you always try to sit on his left. You'll always know when to fold, call or raise. Also, you should try to look at your hand as soon as you can so you can decide if you intend to play it or not. If you're not going to play, don't make an effort to spy his cards. There's no reason to try to find out his hand if you're not going to play. That little bit of extra eye movement or slight turn of the head on your part could give away what you're doing. There's no need to risk it if you're not going to play your hand. And you'd be surprised to see how often it doesn't help to know what your opponent's cards are anyway.

5. Nail Biters

The psychological profile of nail biters is perfect for you. These people are impatient, impulsive and their close decisions are usually wrong.

6. Young Poker Players

By this, I mean players under age 25. Even with the availability of poker books and computers, it's just not likely that a player this young has the experience at the table needed to be a big winner in the long run. If you play with a young player, you can usually be sure he's still learning the game—from you. Even so, this is not as completely true as it used to be. Many, many young players are super-intelligent, have great instincts, and are fearless. Don't make the mistake of underestimating a player just because he's young.

7. Players Who Play Out of a Rack

If you buy in for so many chips that you can't hold them in your hands, then your chips are given to you in a rack at the cashier's cage. Players who bring the rack to the table and play out of the rack instead of taking all of the chips out of the rack really slow up the game. It takes them forever to get the chips out of the rack when it's their turn. A player who is not aware that he's slowing up the game is almost always a beginner and that's exactly who you'd like to play against.

8. Nervous Players

Nervous players always have to be doing something and with so many opportunities to call (every hand), that's what they'll do. They're harder to get out of a pot but you'll beat them in the long run. They are also easy to read and they play too many hands. They often make it very obvious to everyone when they flop a great hand.

9. Rich People

It is more likely than not that the stakes in your game are not high enough to intimidate a rich person. They can afford to take chances and a loss is not as devastating to them as it would be to a less wealthy player in the game. They also are often willing to lose more money than the average player in that game.

10. Seven-Card Stud Players or Recent Converts from the Game

The hand values in the two games are totally different and the seven-card stud player is at a big disadvantage until he learns to reorient his thinking. The two most common mistakes seven-card stud players make are not recognizing when they're drawing dead and overrating pairs in the pocket and going too far with them.

PLAYERS TO AVOID

Everything else being equal, you should prefer not to play with these types of players:

1. Players Who Don't Talk, Smile or Take Their Eyes Off the Game

This type of player is usually tight and experienced enough to know that he should pay attention to the game. The problem with having players like this in your game, is that you won't get any action from him unless he's a favorite to win the hand or already has you beat. If there are more than two players like this in your game, then you can't reasonably expect to win much and you should change games.

2. Drunks

While it's great to be in a game with someone who's drinking, it's terrible to have to play with a drunk. Drunks hold up the game *every time* it's their turn to act, they don't know who has bet or raised, and the action has to be explained to them every time.

3. Older, Retirement-age Players

These players are patient, they wait for high cards, and they don't take chances. Their technical skill is not always that great but they know enough to protect their bankroll. They don't normally have much "gamble" in them and they seldom bluff.

This brings us to what I call *Warren's Rule of Bluffing*. Here's how it works: Assume you are heads-up on the end with an older player who has bet into you and because of the action and the board you can't decide if he's bluffing or not. What you do is quickly estimate that player's age and subtract that number from seventy-five. Whatever number you're left with, that's the percent chance that he's bluffing. You can laugh, but I swear it works in a typical low-limit hold'em game.

4. Sandbaggers

A sandbagger is a player who habitually doesn't bet his hand. He prefers to check-raise and induce bluffs from players who think that a check from him is a sign of weakness. You'll often pay a double bet with a losing hand, but on the other side of the coin, you always know where you stand when he does bet.

5. Other Good Players Beside Yourself

The object of this game is to make money, not to demonstrate your skill or compete with other good players. If you do recognize a good player in your game, you should try to sit on his immediate left. That way he'll always have to act before you do. If he bets, you know you must have slightly better than average cards to call. Since he will often bet more than he'll check, you can use his bet to raise and make the players after you call a double bet more often.

CARD DISTRIBUTION AND PATIENCE

In the long run, you'll be dealt the same cards and get the same flops as every other hold'em player in the world. Even world champion hold'em players like Johnny Chan and Doyle Brunson can't get better cards than you can. You get their cards and flops, and they get yours. The difference, of course, is how you play these cards and flops. The cards don't know if you're winning or losing, although it sometimes seems like they do, and the cards don't know what kind of player you are.

The more you can make your play like that of the world champions, the more money you will win. That's what this book will help you with. The easiest, most immediate thing that a typical low-limit player can do to instantly improve his game is to consistently play only high cards.

This is how many times you can expect to be dealt a particular hand, on average, in an eight-hour hold'em game at thirty-five hands per hour:

FREQUENCY OF HANDS PER POKER SESSION	
8 Hour Game at 35 Hands Per Hour	
Hand	**Frequency**
A-A	None or 1
A-K suited	None or 1
A-K not suited	3 or 4
Any pair	17 or 18
2 suited cards	65 or 66
At least one ace	41 or 42

As you can see, premium hands are few and far between. Also, not all pairs, suited hands, and hands with an ace are playable. You have to make the most of your opportunities.

You're not going to be dealt a pair of aces in the pocket every hand for the rest of your life. There are 169 different possible hands and you're going to get every one of them in the long run. The more hands you play, the more certain it is that all of these hands will be distributed in the expected proportions.

It is likely that you will go through long periods of not getting a playable hand. You will undoubtedly have hours or days or seemingly weeks of getting nothing but K♥ 7♦, Q♣ 5♠, J♠ 2♥ and 7♥ 2♣.

Don't get discouraged. It's normal and you should not let it affect your decisions. The important thing to remember is that your goal is not to play hands of poker, but to make the best decisions hand in and hand out. You're playing to win money, not to play cards, as paradoxical as that sounds.

Frustration results when reality does not meet expectations. If you haven't been dealt a playable hand in two hours and you're feeling frustrated, it's because the reality you're experiencing is not meeting your expectations. It also means you're expecting the wrong thing. You have a quota of playable hands that you expect to be dealt in that two-hour period and you're not meeting it. You had a preconceived idea of how many playable hands you should have gotten, and you didn't get them. What usually happens at this point is that you'll start playing hands you shouldn't because you're more concerned about not playing than you are about making correct decisions.

This is how the expert beats you. He makes his living waiting for you to get tired of waiting for good hands to play. The typical low-limit hold'em player will give in after an hour or so, and start playing anything in an effort to just win a hand. Don't be one of these players. Keep your mind on the true object of the game, which is to consistently make the best decisions in the long run.

If you are being selective about which hands to enter the pot with, as you should be, you won't be playing that many hands to begin with. You already know that the types of hands you are looking for are relatively rare and hard to come by even when the deck is running in your favor. If you're experiencing a bad run of cards, just remember that it will even out in the long run. And you are playing for the long run. That's what enables you to keep an even temperament and not get emotional when you're running good as well as when you're running bad.

Look at these terrible starting hands as an opportunity to save bets where you know other players in your situation would be playing and losing with them.

MNEMONICS

If you can, it's an excellent idea to memorize your two pocket cards and not to look at them again until the hand is over. There is a good reason for doing this. You don't want to give away your hand by having to look at it. Instead, watch the other players and look for tells. You can always check your cards later in the hand if you have to—they'll still be there.

By not looking at your cards, it will prevent you from providing a tell when three of one suit flops. When that happens and players immediately check their hole cards, it usually means that they have exactly one card of that suit and they have to double-check to see which one it is. In low-limit hold'em, this is a very reliable tell. It lets you know that you are facing a four flush but you don't know how high it is.

While we're on the subject of checking your hole cards, you should learn to wait until it's your turn to act to look at your hand. Spend the time before that watching the other players look at their hands. You'll often pick up a tell when someone has been dealt a great hand such as A♦ A♥. It's common in a low-limit game for players to be unaware of the necessity of disguising their reactions to their hands.

Don't look at your hand until the action gets to you.

Your first look at your hand will be more objective and your reaction regarding how to play it will be more involuntary and therefore, less biased. If you look at your hand right away, you give yourself time to change your mind about how to play it, and if you're a typical player, the most common error you'll make is to decide to play it when it's really an unplayable hand.

Many of the pocket hold'em hands have nicknames that help you remember what they are without having to double-check your hand. Here are some:

Hold'em Hand Nicknames

Hand	Nickname	Hand	Nickname
A♣ A♦	- American Airlines	10♠ 2♠	- Doyle Brunson
A♦ K♥	- Big Slick	9♠ 8♥	- Oldsmobile
A♥ J♠	- Ajax	3♥ 9♠	- Jack Benny
A♣ 8♠	- Dead Man's Hand	2♣ 9♥	- Montana Banana, Twiggy
3♣ A♥	- (A♥ 3♣) Baskin Robbins	8♦ 8♥	- Little Oldsmobile
K♥ Q♥	- Marriage	3♣ 8♦	- Raquel Welch
K♠ J♦	- Kojak	7♠ 6♣	- Union Oil
K♦ 9♠	- Canine	6♠ 5♠	- Ken Warren
Q♦ J♥	- Maverick	5♣ 10♦	- Woolworth
Q♣ T♠	- Quint	5♠ 7♣	- Heinz (57 sauce)
Q♠ 7♠	- Computer Hand	4♥ 5♦	- Jesse James Jane Russell
Q♥ 3♥	- San Francisco Busboy (a queen with a trey)	3♦ 3♠	- Crabs
10♣ 4♥	- Broderick Crawford		

SECRETS TO BEATING A LOW-LIMIT GAME

If I could get you aside and I had only five minutes to give you the most important tips about how to beat low-limit poker, the advice below would be it. If you don't read anything else in this chapter, make sure you at least read this list. Everything in this list will be expanded upon later in the book.

Respect Position

This is something that you'll have to consider every time you think about playing a hand for the rest of your poker playing life. It's so important, that it dictates which cards you can play and which cards you can't play. It even makes a hand that's playable in one position unplayable in another position. Generally speaking, you're going to play only very high cards in early position and gradually add more hands that you'll call with as the deal rotates and your position improves.

Avoid Playing Low Cards

While it's true that any two cards can win, it is playing the high cards that will consistently win the money, day in and day out. A hold'em player who consistently plays low cards cannot be a big winner in this game. There are times when it's correct to play low cards, but we'll talk more about that later. Also, several cards that you might consider to be in the medium range are really in the low range. Remember that the odds favor the high cards in the long run.

Realize That it's a Showdown Game

You have to realize that low-limit hold'em is a showdown game and you must adjust accordingly. You are going to have to consistently have the best hand at the end to win. Realize that some players will play anything and they will often play it to the end regardless of any indications that they are beat.

Forget About Bluffing

A lot of low-limit hold'em players are not sophisticated enough to know you may have nothing but are representing a hand. You often won't be able to buy enough pots to make it worth your while to bluff. Somebody will always call to "keep you honest." There are times when it is correct to attempt a bluff but it must be done intelligently, for the right reasons, and under the correct circumstances. This will be covered in detail in a later chapter.

Play Rock-Solid Before the Flop

The most important decision you make every hand is whether or not to get involved to begin with. A bad decision here can, and will, consistently cost you a ton of money. You have to play appropriately for your position and make decisions based on the odds. It is particularly important that you make the correct decision when the pot is raised before the flop since you will be investing a double or triple bet on your hand before you even see the flop. Most players play too loose when making this first decision.

Respect a Raise, Especially Preflop

This goes hand-in-hand with the above advice. There just aren't that many hands that you can profitably play when the pot has been raised preflop. Computer analysis shows that if you can't beat the raiser heads-up at this point, you cannot win money in this situation in the long run. Save your money for those times when *you* want to raise, not when others want to raise.

See the Flop as Cheaply as Possible

There are very few legitimate preflop raising hands in this game. Inexperienced low-limit players often like to build a pot before they see the flop. They often win some of the biggest pots in the game but they also are usually the first ones to bust out of the game. There was a time when the conventional wisdom said to raise preflop with any number of hands (especially A♣ A♦, K♠ K♥ and A♥ K♦) but recent computer analysis proves that it is often more correct to see the flop as cheaply as possible.

Don't Stop Learning the Game

You're not going to learn it all from this book. Talk to other poker players and read as much as you can from poker magazines and good books. See the Cardoza Publishing website for their phenomenal selection of poker books—www.cardozabooks.com—and at a discount!

MY OVERALL PLAN FOR WINNING

Simple. To win the money. This does not mean that you have to play every hand. What it does mean is that you should be a favorite to win the hand when you do play. There are several general principles that you should keep in mind when your goal is to win the money:

1. Always Make the Correct Decision

Your real job is to make the best decisions you can, based on the information available to you at the time. It actually doesn't matter if you win the hand or not. Remember, you can do the wrong thing and still win the hand, but that doesn't prove that you played the hand correctly or that you're a good player.

2. Make Decisions for the Right Reasons

You don't always have to win a certain amount of money in any particular playing session. When you strive for that goal, you start making decisions based on how much money you have in front of you and how big the pot is, instead of relying on odds, tells, and your objective evaluation of what the hand is worth to you.

Every hold'em game has a relative value to you, depending upon the number of players, who the players are, the amount of money on the table, and how long you expect the game to last. Use these factors as your guide in determining how much a game is worth to you.

3. Have a Long-term View of the Game

If you play fifteen hours a week for twenty years, you're going to be dealt about 625,000 hands. You'll be dealt A♥ A♦ more than 2,800 times and you'll get 7♠ 2♦ more than 9,000 times. Your job is to take it all in stride and be rational and not emotional.

You'll have your share of bad beats and sometimes they'll come at the worst times you can imagine. Don't get emotional and go on "tilt." It affects your judgment. Don't live or die over any one hand of poker. It's only one hand and there'll be another one dealt in about a minute.

4. Learn to Recognize a Good Bet

You'll learn that certain hands are consistently profitable while others are big losers before the flop. Likewise, there is usually one best way to play the hand after the flop. With practice, you'll be able to recognize which flops present good bets and which ones are traps.

5. Be Patient

If you're not getting the cards and you're getting impatient to play a hand just because you want to play, remember that you're being tempted to do what you want the other players to do. Don't give in to the temptation to play incorrectly and make decisions that you know are less than your best. Poker is not about what cards you get; it is all about how you play the cards you do get.

6. Play Your Hands Straight Up

That means you should bet when you're strong, check when you're drawing to a straight or flush, and fold when you have nothing. This is an incredibly strong concept that most low-limit players have to learn the hard way. Forget about deception and fancy plays. When you make a completed hand, you can even tell your opponents what you have and they will still call you. I do this when I want to be called by a sole opponent who is about to throw his hand away. He will often call me just because he doesn't believe I would tell the truth.

7

PRACTICAL WINNING HOLD'EM CONCEPTS

THE BLINDS

When choosing a game to play in, the blind structure and the amounts are two things you should consider, even though you won't be able to do anything about them. These factors are already predetermined by the house rules. The player who understands their impact upon the game will be money ahead.

In $1-$4-$8-$8 hold'em, the blinds are $1 and $2, which will cost you a total of $3 per round, assuming you don't call the other dollar when you're the small blind. Since you can play as many as four rounds per hour, the blinds alone will cost you $12 per hour even if you don't play any other hands. If you plan to play for six hours, for example, then you know before you even begin play that you have to make $72 just to break even. In a $3/$6 game, the blinds are $1 and $3, and in a $10/$20 game, the blinds are $5 and $10.

The larger the blinds are, the more it will cost you to play, and of course, the smaller the blinds are, the less it will cost you. This means that the size of the blinds dictate the degree to which you must play conservatively or loosely. If you have a very large blind and play very conservatively, your buy-in will be eaten up by the blinds because you won't be playing any hands. Obviously, that won't work.

On the other hand, imagine that there were no blinds and you entered the pot with only the absolute best hands: A♣ A♦, K♥ K♦, Q♠ Q♣, A♥ K♥, A♦ Q♦, and K♣ Q♣. You'd be able to sit there all day, looking at cards and never risking a dollar unless you had one of these great hands. Theoretically, you could look at 320 hands in eight hours and never pay a dime for the privilege. And if you did enter the pot, you'd be a heavy favorite to win the hand.

So, somewhere between having no blinds and playing for free and having a very large blind and having to play many hands to keep from being blinded to death, there is a happy medium. The blinds determine how loose or tight you should play. The specific advice in later chapters regarding which hands to play in which positions will provide a proper balance between playing too tight or too loose.

When playing the small blind and trying to decide whether or not to call the other dollar, a good rule of thumb is this: Don't limp in to see the flop for the other dollar unless you have a hand that you would voluntarily pay $2 for.

All too often a player will have something like J♠ 6♠ in the small blind, call the other $1, make a good hand in a huge pot and then lose the hand along with a good portion of his chips. And what's the first thing he says? "Damn, I never would have called with that hand, except it only cost me one more dollar." If you wouldn't pay $2 for it, don't pay $1 more for it, either.

Of course there's an exception to every rule. An exception here would be if almost everyone has called and you have a hand that is not that great in itself, but has the potential to make the nuts if you get the right flop. Some examples of this type of hand would be A♣ 5♦, J♥ 7♠, 10♣ 8♥, 8♥ 5♠, 7♥ 6♣ and especially 6♠ 5♦.

Here's a miscellaneous thought about playing in the

blind. The blind will always have an average, random hand. If the pot has been raised preflop and there are a lot of callers and you get a non-descript flop like…

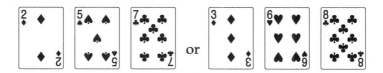

…beware if the blind bets it right out, for these reasons: He's in the worst of all possible positions, he's betting into a large field, he's betting into raisers and he knows he's going to be called. It's been my experience that the blind has a great hand in this situation, even though it was statistically unlikely before the flop. Usually, the blind has flopped two pair or even a set when this situation occurs.

SEATING TIP

Here's a good seating tip that saves me a lot of money in the long run. If you're a fairly conservative player and you don't like to have your blinds raised, then sit to the right of the oldest player in the game if you can. In typical games, the older players usually like to see the flop as cheaply as possible, even when they have A♦ A♥, K♣ K♠ or A♦ K♦ in the pocket. They like to see the flop before they put any real money in the pot or take any chances in the hand. And if you do get a raise from this player, you'll always know where you stand. Give him credit for a super hand.

STRADDLING

Sometimes the player to the immediate left of the big blind, for example in a $1-$4-$8-$8 game, will put $4 in the pot before he even gets his cards. This is called a **straddle**. What he is doing, in effect, is raising the big blind $2 "in the dark." This raise has the effect of creating three blinds ($1 / $2 / $4) and does not count against the maximum number of raises allowed. When the action comes back around to the straddle, he then has the option of raising himself and this time his raise does count against the maximum number of raises allowed.

This is what you should keep in mind when playing against a straddle:

- The straddle will have a random hand since he raised before he saw his hand. Statistically speaking, his median hand will be around a Q♣ 6♠. That means that half of his hands will be better than that, and half will be worse than that.

- You should pass ordinary drawing hands such as J♣ 10♦ and Q♥ 9♠ and play only premium hands.

- You should come in raising if you decide to play. The $4 straddle plus your $4 raise will give you leverage to drive out the other players behind you and go heads-up with the straddle. This will pit your excellent hand against the straddle's random hand and gives you the best chance to win the pot. If other players have called to see the flop, you should still be a favorite in the hand.

- If another player reraises behind you, then you are usually facing a genuinely powerful hand and you should revert back to your usual strategy.

- Don't ever straddle the blinds yourself. You're just giving your money away for no good reason.

THE RAKE

Theoretically, poker is a zero-sum game. Your loss is another player's gain. The total amount of money put into the game remains the same, it just gets redistributed as the game goes on. If ten players with $100 each sit in a game it is possible for one player to eventually win all $1,000.

But that's not possible when you play in a casino because of the "rake." The **rake** is a percentage of the pot that the casino takes out of each pot to compensate it for the cost of providing the dealers, chips, poker table, and all the other overhead. If you play long enough in a raked game, the house will eventually have all the money. Now, instead of one player winning the $1,000, the house will win the money—$2, $3 or $4 at a time—in three or four hundred hands.

An excellent example of the impact of the rake on a game occurred when the President Casino opened in Biloxi, Mississippi in August, 1992. There was a $15/$30 and/or a $20/$40 hold'em game nearly every day. The games were full most of the time and the rake was $5 maximum per hand.

In a big-limit game like that, it was easy to build a $50 pot to qualify for the $5/$10 percent max rake. Well, at forty hands per hour for an average of twenty hours per day, the house was taking $4,000 per day out of the game. That's $28,000 per week, per table. This money was lost forever and would never again be available to the players to put into the game.

Soon the game started later and later in the day, it broke up earlier and earlier at night, it began to be spread short-handed and eventually there weren't enough players with enough money to start the game at all. The same thing started all over again with a $10/$20 game and when there weren't enough players with enough money to keep that game going, the same thing started all over again with a $5/$10 game. By spring 1994, they hardly ever had a hold'em game at all. If, instead, they offered a hold'em game with a $2 maximum rake, they would have filled every hold'em table every day.

The rake is taken out of the winner's pot. Remember that every time you enter a pot you're exposing yourself to the house rake, the jackpot drop and the dealer's toke if you win the hand. You need to play pretty good poker to beat all that and nine other players too.

14 CATEGORIES OF STARTING HANDS

Knowing the categories of starting hands will not in itself make you money or save you money. What it will do is serve to remind you what type of hand you have and what type of hand you are looking to make. It will also remind you of the limitations of your hand and hopefully keep you from losing too much money in the wrong situations. Two good examples of what I'm talking about would be expecting to make a straight when you have K♥ K♠ in the pocket or expecting to make a heart or diamond flush when you have J♥ 10♦ in the pocket.

Here are the 14 categories of starting hands that you should be aware of:

1. High Pairs

A♣ A♦, K♥ K♠, Q♦ Q♣. You will always be a favorite with these cards and you usually want to raise preflop. You will win bigger pots when you have the best cards and you'll drive out the garbage hands that might occasionally draw out on you. It's a sin to limp in with A♥ A♣ and get beat by someone holding 7♠ 4♠, especially after the hand when he's dragging the pot and says, "I wouldn't have played if you had raised before the flop."

2. Medium Pairs

J♦ J♥, 10♠ 10♣, 9♣ 9♦, 8♥ 8♣. You might be surprised to see that a pair of jacks in the pocket is considered to be a medium pair, and not a high one. The fact is that if you have J♦ J♣ in the pocket, you will get a queen, king or ace (an overcard) on the flop 57 percent of the time.

3. Low Pairs

7♠ 7♥, 6♦ 6♣, 5♥ 5♦, 4♣ 4♦, 3♥ 3♠, 2♦ 2♣. When you have 7♥ 7♣ in the pocket, you'll flop one or more overcards 92 percent of the time. So what you're really looking for is to flop a set or an open-end straight draw. An excellent flop for 7♥ 7♣ would be 6♠ 5♥ 4♦ or 8♣ 6♦ 5♥. The fact that you hold not one but two sevens makes it 33 percent less likely that anyone else will be holding one also to create a split pot if you make the straight. You normally cannot win a big pot with these hands if you don't improve on the flop.

You should try to see the flop as cheaply as possible since you will *not* improve most of the time. One overcard on the flop does not always kill your hand but the problem is knowing when to continue playing or when to let the hand go. The most important considerations are the number of players in to see the flop against you and what the overcard is.

A flop of A♥ 6♠ 2♣ with seven players seeing the flop makes your hand unquestionably unplayable when you hold 7♥ 7♣, while a flop of 8♦ 6♣ 2♥ against one opponent is not as threatening. This is especially true if your sole opponent raised preflop, indicating he does not hold an 8, even though he might have a premium pair in the pocket.

By the way, if you hold 3♣ 3♠ and flop 6♠ 5♥ 4♦, get the hell out. A draw to the low end of a straight is one of the classic sucker plays in hold'em and you won't be a winner in the long run if you normally attempt draws like that. An exception would be if there was no bet on the flop and you caught a deuce on the turn. Now, your hand is a lot better because you actually do have a straight, and that beats a higher straight draw in the long run.

4. Nut Flush Draws

Any card with a suited ace. You'll have the nuts if you make the flush, the board doesn't pair and if no straight flushes are possible.

The value of the non-ace card has a serious impact on your chances of winning the hand also, especially if you miss the flush draw. For example, A♥ K♥ will win about 24 percent of the time while A♥ 2♥ will win only about 11 percent of the time. This is because when you miss the flush but pair your odd card, a pair of kings will win more hands than a pair of deuces. Keep this in mind: Starting with two suited cards, you will *not* make a flush 97 percent of the time.

5. King-High Flush Draws

K♣ Q♣ down through K♣ 2♣. The odds of making the flush are the same as with the A♣ Q♣, but the problem is when you actually make the flush. It's a real chip bleeder when you make a flush holding K♠ J♠ and you get raised and lose a big pot to someone holding A♠ 3♠. The good news is that one-third of the time you do make the flush, the ace of your suit will be on the board (giving you the nut flush) and when you make a king-high flush, you will often have the best hand because the ace of your suit is just not in play this hand.

Be especially careful when you make a flush holding K♦ Q♦ and you are raised or reraised. For you to have the best hand at this point, your opponent would have to be raising you with, at best, a jack-high flush. You have to ask yourself, "Would he play the hand this way with just a jack-high flush knowing that I could have the queen, king or ace-high flush?" Most of the time in this situation you'll find that you're beat by the ace-high flush. If you really know your opponent, you could even throw the hand away, saving one or two bets on the end.

6. Ace-High Suited

A♣ K♣, A♦ Q♦, A♥ J♥. Most of the time you win a pot with one of these hands, it will be because you made a pair of aces and your kicker held up, or you made aces-up. You will make a flush with these hands only 3 percent more often than you would if they weren't suited. Any ace-high straight draw you have with these hands will always be a gutshot.

The beauty of this hand is that you can miss your straight or flush draw and still win the hand by making a big pair. Occasionally, ace-high will be the best hand at the end. You should usually play the hand as if it were not suited until you see the flop. An exception would be if you were last and a lot of players have limped in to see the flop. In this case I would raise to build a pot in the event I hit my hand. With no preflop raise, you probably have the best hand at that point anyway and you figure to win more than your share of pots in the long run.

7. Ace-Medium Suited
A♦ 10♦, A♠ 9♠, A♥ 8♥, A♣ 7♣. With this hand, you are really hoping to make either aces up or a flush. If you make a pair of aces, you'll find that your kicker is usually no good if there's any other interest in the pot at all. Do not play this hand heads-up if there's a raise preflop because you don't figure to beat the raiser in the long run and you don't have the proper odds to draw to a flush. You're about a 4-1 underdog to any other player holding an ace with a higher kicker than yours.

Ace-medium suited is a vastly overrated hand by typical low-limit players and you should invest as little as possible in it until you see the flop. This hand is best played in late position with a lot of callers already in the pot. This also applies to A♦ 6♦, A♥ 5♥, A♠ 4♠, A♣ 3♣ and A♦ 2♦.

8. Ace-Face
A♣ K♦, A♥ Q♠, A♦ J♠. These are the bread-and-butter cards of Texas hold'em. You'll get these cards three times as often unsuited as suited and they're usually played pretty aggressively preflop and on the flop. The most common

hand you'll make with these cards is a pair of aces with a good kicker. If you pair your face card, you'll always have the best kicker (your ace). If you make a straight, it will be the nuts if you use both cards (barring flush or full house possibilities).

9. Ace-Medium and Ace-Low

A♣ 10♦, A♦ 9♥, A♥ 8♠, A♠ 7♣, A♣ 6♠, A♦ 5♥, A♥ 4♦, A♠ 3♥ and A♣ 2♠. These are the most costly trap hands in low-limit hold'em and you should routinely muck them every time you get them.

If you flop an ace, your kicker will almost always not be any good. In a ten-handed low-limit game, where most every player plays every ace he's dealt, you can safely assume that if an ace comes on the flop, it has made someone a pair of aces. When you have an ace in the pocket, there will be an ace dealt to at least one other player 74.7 percent of the time. If his kicker is better than yours, then you are a 4-1 underdog and if your kicker is worse than his, then you won't win much from him or you'll have a split pot.

10. Face-Face

K♠ Q♥, K♥ J♦, Q♥ J♠. You have the nut straight draw and your main concern is that you don't flop an overcard. If you have K♦ Q♥ or K♠ J♦, you will flop one or two aces 23 percent of the time, and if you have Q♥ J♣, you will flop one or more aces or kings an incredible 41 percent of the time. This hand does best when you use both pocket cards to make a straight.

11. Any Two Suited Cards

Suited cards not already mentioned, such as K♠ 7♠, Q♥ 5♥, 9♣ 3♣. These hands are played almost purely for the flush draw. When you start suited you will flop two more cards of your suit only 10.94 percent of the time—that's 8-1 against. And after you flop the four flush, you'll make the flush only 35 percent of the time. This type of hand is a favorite of a lot of low-limit players and it is a hand that you should encourage your opponents to play.

You will never have the right odds to play the hand for any reason and it is a big loser. If you are a good player, this is the type of hand that the other players will be holding when you beat them. Your job is to smile, drag the pot and say, "Nice hand."

12. Two Connected Cards

Hands not already mentioned, such as 10♠ 9♦, 7♣ 6♥ or 5♦ 4♣. Your goal is to make a straight and you should only play these hands in late position when there are a lot of callers and no raises preflop. If you pair one of your cards on the flop, such as holding 6♥ 5♣ and you get a 5♥ on the flop, you'll get another 5 by the river only 10.9 percent of the time. These are terrible odds to fight in the long run and you often won't win the hand even if you do make trips.

13. Suited and Connected

Cards such as 9♠ 8♠, 7♥ 6♥ or 5♣ 4♣. These hands are only marginally better than the same hand unsuited. You have only an extra 3 percent chance of making a flush and when you do it's only 8 or 9 high. You should see the flop as cheaply as possible with this hand, play it only in late position with many players, and be careful if you make the flush. Oddly enough, you would rather make a straight than a flush with this hand because you can make a nut straight but you can never make a nut flush, unless it's a straight flush.

14. J♥ 10♣

In the early 1970s when Texas hold'em was gaining popularity, an influential poker writer made a comment something like this: "Of all the possible hands that I could hold in a full game of hold'em, I would choose J♥ 10♣, suited or not. It makes the nut straight five different ways, it fits in with the cards immediately above and below it, and the only way you don't get some piece of the flop is if the flop is all low cards, which is unlikely. I actually prefer it to A♦ A♥ in a full game."

Since there weren't that many hold'em books on the market at that time, he was able to influence the thinking of a whole generation of hold'em players and his sentiment on the subject is popularly believed by most low-limit players today. I want to tell you that computer analysis has shown J♣ 10♦ to be a vastly overrated hand and it is only marginally profitable in most circumstances. You should usually not play this hand in early position and play carefully with it until you see the flop.

KEY STARTING HAND CONCEPTS

Generally speaking, you should think of all your starting hands as being one of two types of hands:

1. Big cards that will stand up with little improvement against a small field.

2. Cards that are a draw to a straight or a flush where you would prefer to play against a large field so you would win a big pot if you do hit your hand.

The first thing you should do when looking at your first two cards is to classify them as either a folding, calling or raising hand, depending on your position. Ask yourself if you would rather play this hand against one or ten players. The answer to that question will tell you what you want to do when the action comes to you.

Keep in mind that players who entered the pot before you are not likely to fold when you raise before the flop. On the other hand, the earlier your position is, the more players you will knock out when you raise before their turn, because now they have to call two bets. If you just call, then your money in the pot encourages more calls behind you and you should have a hand you prefer to play with many players to see the flop. The earlier your position is, the stronger your hand has to be because of the possibility of raises behind you.

One sure way to tell if you're playing hands too weak for your position is by how you instantly and involuntarily react when you've limped in an early position and it's raised behind you. If you don't mind, then you're probably playing good cards for your position. But if it's raised and you're cussing the raiser under your breath, then you should take that as a hint that you're playing too loose for your position.

When you raise with big cards in the pocket, you're limiting the size of the final pot, but you're increasing your chances of winning the hand. In a ten-handed game, you will win 10 percent of the hands, on average. In a two-handed game you will win 50 percent of the hands, on average. Limping in and allowing a large field to see the flop, or raising to get it heads-up, is a trade-off between pot size and chance of winning the hand.

Hold'em hands are not only valuable for how much money they can earn you, but they are also valuable for how much money they can save you. Compare A♦ A♥ with A♠ K♣.

Let's say that you win 100 total bets with each hand. With A♦ A♥ you lose 40 bets to other hands for a net win of 60 bets. With A♠ K♣ in the pocket, you win the same 100 bets as with A♦ A♥, but because you don't make anything on the flop, you throw it away and you lose only 30 bets with it for a net win of 70 bets.

The problem (if there is one) with A♦ A♥ in the pocket is that after the flop you still have at least a pair of aces to continue playing with. That's not true with A♠ K♣ and that's what makes it easier to lose less money with it. That is why, in my opinion, A♠ K♣ is sometimes more valuable to me than a pair of aces in the pocket.

This same line of reasoning applies to hands like 5♠ 4♠ and 5♥ 4♦. You can make your flush and lose a lot of money but the hand is easier to throw away if it's not suited and you don't flop anything.

One way to decide for yourself if you have a good hand or not after the flop is to try this simple exercise.

1. Look at your hand and ask yourself what kind of flop or flops you would like to see.

2. Now look at the flop without considering what you just did and ask yourself what kinds of hands would go well with a flop like this.

If you find that the flop fits your hand and your hand fits the flop, then you have an excellent hand. If the flop doesn't fit your hand and/or your hand doesn't fit the flop, then you might have a problem hand and you certainly shouldn't bet money on it. Wait for a better hand. You should get in the habit of doing this with every hand you play.

Your hand is even stronger when you use both of your pocket cards to make your poker hand. You will usually have the best hand and another player will need to have the exact same cards as you just to have a split pot.

Look at this example of the power of using both of your hole cards: You have K♥ J♣ in the pocket and the board is Q♦ 10♠ 9♥ 8♣ 3♥. You have the nuts and you don't even have to worry about a split pot because another player would have to be holding exactly a king and a jack. The odds are always against another player holding exactly the two specific cards he needs to beat or tie you.

But what if that last card, the 3♥, came instead the K♣? Now, all anyone would need to split the pot with you would be a jack, and it's pretty likely that someone is holding one, given the flop. You're more likely to have a split pot because you're using only one of your cards, the J♣, and it's easy for anyone to hold just a jack.

POSITION

Understanding the importance of position is so critical in this game that it means the difference between winning and losing with the same cards. Hands that are playable and are winners in late position are often unplayable and losers in earlier positions.

If you are first, second or third to act after the dealer, then you are said to be in **early position**. This is also called being **up front**. If you are the dealer, or one or two seats to the right of the dealer, then you are in **late position**. The players after early position and before late position (and normally sitting directly across the table from the dealer) are in **middle position**.

Not all poker hands are created equal and their relative values depends on your position. K♥ 9♥ in the first seat after the big blind is worth a lot less than if you had the same hand in last position. When you play that type of hand (or any hand) up front, you can never be sure if there will be a raise behind you or not, forcing you to play the hand for two bets or more when it is worth only one bet.

What they say are the three most important things regarding real estate (location, location and location), also applies to hold'em—position, position and position.

Position is so important that it is the one thing that you will have to take into consideration when deciding whether or not to play each hand of poker that you are going to play for the rest of your poker-playing life. Your position is so important that it is the major factor that determines when you can play a hand and when you can't.

You need to know, before calling that initial bet, how many players before you have called and how many players after you might call or raise behind you. The more players left to act behind you, the more likely it is that there will be a raise. This is true for all forms of poker but it is especially true for hold'em because hold'em, when correctly played, is an aggressive, raising game.

75

Each player in turn behind you can correctly play progressively weaker and weaker hands because there are fewer players behind him who might raise. The number of potential raisers is reduced with each player who passes or calls. If you have a weak, or less than a premium hand, you certainly would rather see the flop for only one bet than for two bets or more.

Your position in hold'em is also important because it does not change during the course of the hand. Being first to act for four betting rounds is a distinct disadvantage because you normally have no idea how many players will call or raise behind you until it happens. On the other hand, being last to act for four consecutive betting rounds is one of the biggest advantages you could have without everybody actually showing you their cards. By the time the action gets to you they will have, in effect, shown you their cards anyway. You will at least know how they feel about their hands by the way they have checked, bet, raised or reraised with their hands.

If you're last, every player in the game will have to act on his hand for four rounds without knowing what you're going to do. You, on the other hand, won't have to act on your hand until you've seen what everyone else has done with theirs. When you're last to act, you're in a powerful position. You can save money by folding when someone else has called a bet ahead of you, or you can raise when you have the best hand.

EARLY POSITION

When you are in early position, the type of hands that you can play is restricted to:

1. High cards, hands that clearly have a high expectation of winning.

2. Hands that will win with little or no improvement.

3. Drawing cards like A♥ Q♥, hands that still have a chance to win if you miss your draw. You can miss your heart draw and still win with a pair of aces or queens.

The hands you play up front should be able to stand a raise behind you if it comes. These are the only hands that you can profitably play from early position in a low-limit game:

Early Position Hands

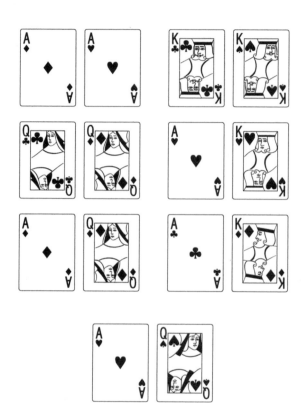

As you become a more experienced hold'em player and gain a deeper insight into the subtleties of the game, there are several other hands that you can add to this early position starting hand list. This is also true for the following middle and late position starting hand list and these added hands will be covered later.

Anything else, no matter how pretty it looks, is not profitable played in an early position in a low-limit game.

MIDDLE POSITION

While playing in middle position, you will usually have a few callers in front of you already in the pot and you'll have a few more potential callers behind you. Because the chance of a raise is somewhat reduced and there are already several players in the pot, you are getting better odds to play somewhat weaker hands and you will often be getting the correct odds to play drawing hands like J♣ 10♣.

Also realize that if you call, it raises the pot odds for the players behind you and makes it more correct for them to play weaker hands. **Pot odds** are the odds that the pot is offering you in relation to the size of the bet you are making or calling. For example, if a sole opponent bets $10 into a $50 pot (to create a $60 pot), then you are getting pot odds of 6 to 1. If you think your odds of winning a hand if you call are better than 6 to 1, then you should call. If you think your odds of winning the hand if you call are less than 6 to 1, then you should not call.

For example, a player who is last with 10♠ 9♥ cannot play if there are only one or two players in the pot. He just doesn't have the right odds to draw to the hand. But if you call in middle position with something like K♦ 10♦, you might have induced the player on your left to call because he has one more player in the pot (you) and the pot is slightly bigger. This, in turn, starts a domino effect where each player calls a bigger pot and adds one bet to it. The last player might be getting 6 to 1 on his bet and can *now* play his 10♠ 9♥.

The effect of calling in early and middle position is that it induces players to play weaker hands behind you, especially in low-limit hold'em. This increases the size of the pot if you win, but it reduces your overall chances of winning the pot to begin with.

Here is the list of hands that you can play in middle position, in addition to the Early Position list:

Middle Position Hands

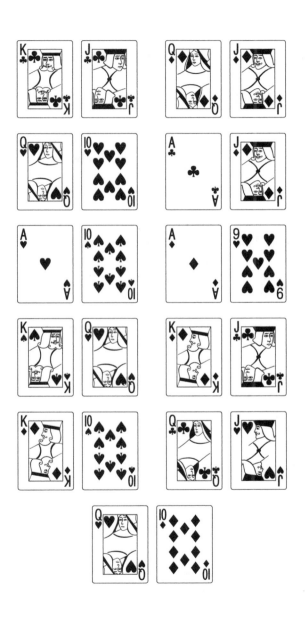

LATE POSITION AND
PLAYING THE BUTTON

When you have the button, it simply means that you are in the dealer's position and will be the last to act on each round of betting on that hand. As mentioned earlier, being last to act for four consecutive betting rounds is a major advantage because you'll be the most informed player in the game. Another big advantage is that if there were no raises, then only the blinds can raise the pot.

Here's an "on the button" tip: If you have a genuine borderline calling hand and you would play it only if you knew the blinds would not raise, then this is what you should do. Pause when the action gets to you and take a look to see what the blinds are doing. Most of the time in low-limit hold'em the blinds will not be aware of the importance of concealing their intentions. They will often already have their chips in hand, ready to raise, when the option gets back around to them. Does he have in his hand the correct number of chips to raise or does he have his hand ready to tap the table in a checking motion? Sometimes, the blind will actually say "check" while waiting for you to act on your hand.

The most important thing to keep in mind when playing the button is not to play hands just because you're on the button. This is where too many low-limit players lose too much of their money. They get trapped with hands that they have absolutely no business playing. Too many players think they can play any hand they want and can get in for only one bet. If it's incorrect to play a hand, the fact that you can play it for only one bet and you can play it on the button doesn't make the hand any better. You should not play any hand on the button that you wouldn't play one or two seats to the right it.

The secret to playing the button is to realize that it does not increase the odds of your cards making the best hand just because you are last to act. It does not change ordinarily losing hands into winners. At best, being on the button allows you to limp in with hands that you would not want to call a raise with. After that, it lets you get in an extra bet when you want to or your hand warrants.

While we're on the subject of playing the button, there is a tell that is related to the button that I have found to be very reliable, especially in low-limit hold'em. When a player is last to act and he starts handling, moving or otherwise adjusting the button, it usually means he intends to call just because he's on the button. The value of this tell is in the fact that it tells you what he *doesn't* have, rather than what he does have.

A player who has A♦ A♥, K♥ K♣, Q♠ Q♦ or A♣ K♠ on the button will be very still and not make any movements that will draw attention to himself. He's going to be so intent on watching the action as it comes to him that he may not even put his cards down, let alone play with the button. He almost certainly does not have two high cards in the pocket and he probably has something that he considers to be a garbage hand but he's going to play just because he's on the button. You can usually treat him like a blind hand unless you have evidence otherwise.

The hands that you can play in late position, including the Early Position list and the Middle Position list are:

Late Position Hands

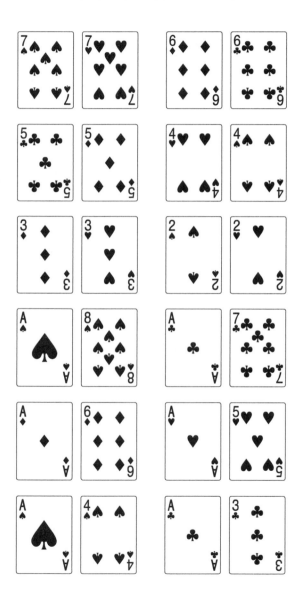

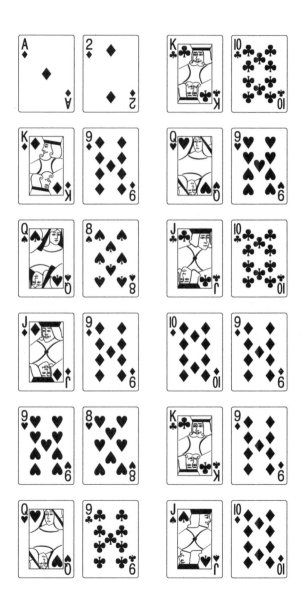

These aren't the only hands you'll ever play in hold'em. They're just the only ones that will show a profit for their position in the long run. In a ten-handed game you'll be in the blind 20 percent of the time and that's when you'll get to play most of the other hands.

Just like it's important to play cards appropriate for your position, it's important that you don't get in the habit of playing cards that are not appropriate for your position. The most common example you'll see in a low-limit game of playing out of position is to see a player play a hand in early position just because it's on his list of hands to play in late position. He thinks it's okay to play Q♦ 8♥ in the first seat after the big blind just because he plays the same hand on the button. In other words, he totally disregards his position when electing to play a hand.

This is one way that you make your profit from this game. Your profit comes from the mistakes your opponents make. You'll suffer some bad beats from players playing bad cards in bad positions but if you consistently make the right decisions and have a long-term view of the game, you'll get 'em in the end.

ALL-IN STRATEGIES

You should be aware of the fact when you or another player don't have enough checks to play a hand all the way to the end of the hand, and therefore, will have to go all in. If you're not going to buy more checks and know you'll probably have to go all in on the next hand you play, then you should choose that hand as carefully as you can considering how many hands you can look at before the big blind gets to you. Here are several important tips to keep in mind if you might go all in.

1. Eliminate Players

You should come in raising to cut down on the number of players against you. Even though you may have a premium hand you should be more concerned about winning the hand rather than winning a big pot.

2. If Another Player Beside Yourself Is About to Go All in

You should consider betting or raising to ensure he does go all in, even if, and especially if, you think he has you beat. Getting him all in does three good things for you:

> **a.** If he has you beat, then you have started building a side pot for yourself that he cannot win. The earlier in the hand that you start to build a side pot, the more money you will win if you win the hand.

> **b.** If he does not have you beat and he does not win any of the main pot, then he will have to either buy-in for more money or leave the game and give the seat to a new player who will have a full buy-in. Both of these events have the effect of getting more money on the table and into the game, which is good for you.

> **c.** Your bet or raise may have the unintended side effect of driving out a player who might have beat you had you not bet or raised.

3. Heads-up

When you get a player all in heads-up against you, you have a special problem. Depending on what you think he has, you might want to leave him with enough checks so that he will consider throwing his hand away on the flop. For example, you have A♥ A♠, you raise preflop and your sole opponent reraises you, leaving him only $4 left to play the hand with. Ordinarily, you'd want to reraise to get him all in, but you might want to wait to see the flop, because once you do get him all in, he gets to play the hand all the way to the river for free. If he gets a terrible flop, he might change his mind about going all in and save his last $4 when you bet on the flop.

I learned this lesson the hard way—twice. I had A♥ A♠ in the pocket, got my sole opponent all in before the flop, and flopped A♣ K♦ Q♠. If I had left him checks to play with, he would have thrown the hand away when I bet on the flop, because all he had was 2♥ 2♣ and he was certain I had flopped a set of aces, kings or queens, or aces-up. Since he was all in and couldn't fold his pair of deuces, he won the pot when the turn was the 2♦ and the river was the 2♠ for four of a kind.

The other time I had A♠ A♣ in the pocket and got my only opponent all in preflop. The flop was A♥ 7♦ 5♦. If he had any money at all and had to call a bet, he would have thrown his hand away on the flop. But instead, he got to see the Q♣ and the J♠ come on the turn and river for free and it fit in perfectly with his K♥ 10♣ to make the nut straight. Both of these lessons were expensive, since I was playing $20/$40 limit both times.

4. Avoid a Side Pot

You should usually not try to create a side pot if you think you might not have the first- or second-best hand in the game. The first- and second-best hands will win the main pot and the side pot. If that's not you, then you're just wasting your money. If you create a side pot when you didn't have to and then you miss your hand, you'll usually have to bluff at the side pot. And if you win that, you'll still have to show your hand to the guy who went all in for the main pot. Remember, since he probably chose to go all in on this hand, he probably has a better hand than average himself.

5. You Will Win More Hands than Average

When you do choose to go all in, typically, you will have chosen a better hand than average to play and, more importantly, you will get to play the hand all the way to the end without having to fold. An excellent example would be if you had 10♥ 10♣ in the pocket. The flop was J♣ 6♦ 5♣, and there was a bet and two raises. You would certainly throw away your hand because there are so many reasonable hands that could beat you, given the bet and two raises. They are any pair in the pocket higher than jacks, A♣ J♦, K♥ J♠, Q♦ J♦, 6♣ 6♠ and 5♥ 5♠. You'll get another 10 by the river one out of nine times and win a pot that you never would have played if you had to pay.

6. Protect Your Bankroll

Choosing to go all in is a critical decision if you must win the hand to stay in the game. Protect your bankroll, no matter how small it is. Don't play a hand just for the sake of getting rid of your last $8 or $10, or whatever you have left. Just $5, when played judiciously, can rapidly put you back in the game if you win. If you go all in with $5 against four other players and win, you will have $25 to play with. If you go all in with that $25 against four players and win, you'll have $125.

This, of course, does not take into account the effect of the rake, jackpot drop, and dealer tokes, or the size of the pots you win—but you get the idea. Choose your all-in hands with care because it means the difference between winning and losing this playing session. Try to keep enough money on the table so you don't have to go all in, if possible.

IF YOU CAN'T WIN THIS HAND...

Often you will have doubts about a hold'em hand as it progresses from the flop and into the turn and river, and it becomes apparent that you won't win the hand you're playing. All is not lost, however. Depending upon your position, the number of players left in the hand, who the players are, and what the flop is, you can sometimes, but not that often, influence the outcome of the hand.

An ideal situation would be if you were to see the turn card with two other players, one a drinking player who plays badly, and the other an older, conservative player who doesn't take chances. The turn card comes and you're sure you can't win the hand. When the loose player bets, you raise, even though your hand doesn't warrant it. This makes the tight player call two big bets on the turn and in all probability, he'll muck his cards unless he has a really great hand. The bad player then wins the hand on the river.

The reason this helps you is that you can get that money back from the bad player. The tight player who wins a big pot is more likely to hold on to the money and not lose it back nearly as fast as any other player at the table (beside yourself, of course).

If you must lose a hand, you should not mind losing to any one of the players that you would like to play against (listed earlier). When you lose a pot to a player who is not as good a player as you are, you should consider that money to be just a temporary loan. It may take an hour, a day or a week, but your superior play will get that money back in the long run.

> When you lose a pot to a player who is not as good a player as you are, you should consider that money to be just a temporary loan.

There are three additional types of players that you shouldn't mind losing a pot to once in a while:

1. Players Who Have Just Been Seated

You shouldn't mind losing to players that have not played for long. Most players stay for quite a while when they decide to take a seat in a poker game and a player who wins a big pot right after he sits down will probably stay long enough for you to have a chance to win it back. It's rare that a player will sit down in a hold'em game, win a big pot and immediately leave the game. You'll have plenty of opportunities to get that money back.

2. The Worst Player in the Game

The reason is obvious, but sometimes it takes longer to get your money back because the worst player will play nearly every hand against you. You'll have to have the best hand at the showdown nearly every time and if that's the only way you can win, it will take a little longer.

3. The Player on Your Right

You would rather lose a pot to the player on your right than the one on your left. Since the player on your right will have acted on his hand before you do, you'll almost always have position on him. The money on the table tends to move clockwise in hold'em because of position, and the idea is for his money to move clockwise into your stack.

If possible, you should sit to the left of bad players, players who play too many hands, players who have a lot of money in front of them, and players who bet more often than their hands warrant. And if you can find a player who has more than one of these qualities, then so much the better for you.

TO PLAY OR NOT TO PLAY A HAND?

How do you, after looking at your two pocket cards, decide whether or not to play the hand? What makes you call the blind and raises, and what makes you throw the hand away? Here's how I look at the question.

Assume you are playing in your usual hold'em game. That's easy to imagine. I'm going to ask you to imagine a lot more after this, so pay close attention. Assume that you are in your typical game with your typical number of players, with the usual stakes that you play for and so on. Now you look down to see that you have been dealt Q♣ 9♥. If you don't like Q♣ 9♥ as your hand, then feel free to mentally substitute any other hand that you like for this example. It doesn't matter.

In fact, this exercise is meant for every two-card combination, because you will be dealt every two-card combination in the long run.

After the flop, assume that you play the hand as you see fit. You can throw the hand away, you can call, or raise, or do anything you want. Now comes the tricky part. Assume that you will get this same hand dealt to you for the next one million hands; that this is the only hold'em hand that you'll ever be dealt for the rest of your life. (I hope you picked a good one.) You'll get the hand in every position under all the usual game conditions. Every time you get Q♣ 9♥ (or whatever hand you've chosen), you do not remember what the hand was after it's over, and neither does anyone else.

Now, assuming all of this, which I admit is a lot, the question is: After playing this hand for one million consecutive hands under all circumstances, are you winning or losing? One million hands is long enough for winning and losing streaks to run their course and for everything statistical to average out in the long run. The answer to the question, "Am I winning or losing?" is also the answer to the question, "Do I play this hand or not?" Simple, isn't it?

Any hand that wins money in the long run is said to have a **positive expectation**. Any hand that loses money in the long run is said to have a **negative expectation**. A hand that neither wins nor loses in the long run is said to have a **zero expectation**. You normally don't want to play hands that have a negative expectation, with the exception of changing up your play for deception or advertising purposes (which will be covered later).

Knowing your expectation of winning will help you decide how to play difficult hands in different situations and positions, and will guide you in your play on the flop, turn and river. This reasoning, combined with an understanding of pot odds and drawing odds, will enable you to make sound decisions based on logic. Most of the decisions that you will make in a low-limit hold'em game will be based on your knowledge of mathematics, probability, tells and pot odds.

EXPECTATION PRINCIPLES

Every hand of poker that you play will have either a positive, negative or zero expectation, depending on the odds you are getting in the hand. What that means is that you're not guaranteed to win any hand in particular, but if you play the hand over and over, you will either win or lose with it, and your expectation per hand is your win or loss divided by the number of times you played the hand.

For example, if you played the Q♣ 9♥ hand one million times and found that you had won exactly one million dollars, then your expectation would be a positive $1 per hand. I'll explain each type of expectation in detail, beginning with zero expectation.

Zero expectation is when the pot odds are exactly the same as the drawing odds. I'll start with simple examples and gradually move toward showing you how this applies to poker. I'll start by offering you a proposition bet. You and I are going to flip a fair coin one million times and every time it comes up heads, I will pay you $1, and every time it comes up tails, you will pay me $1.

At the end of our one million trials, how do you think we will stand, money-wise? The fact is that since a fair coin is as likely to come up heads as tails, you could expect the coin to come up heads approximately 500,000 times and it would come up tails approximately 500,000 times. We would be even.

Two Stacks

Now, using a deck of cards and about 50 poker chips, we are going to perform the following exercises. Divide the poker chips into two equal stacks, one on your left representing red, and the other on your right representing black. You're going to bet one chip each on whether the top card off the deck is red or black. Put one chip in the middle from each stack and turn the top card. It it's a red card, award the two-chip pot to the red stack on your left. If it's black, then award the pot to the black stack on your right.

Zero Expectation Example

Now put a chip from each stack in the pot and turn the second card in the deck. Award the pot to the winner and repeat this procedure with all of the remaining deck, until the deck is gone. As you might have suspected by now, each player has exactly as many chips as he started out with. That's because it is equally likely that, in the absence of any other information, the top card off any deck of cards is as likely to be red as black.

Now let's get a little more complicated.

Divide your chips into four equal stacks, playing one for yourself and the other three for three imaginary opponents. The names of your imaginary opponents are Club, Diamond and Heart. Your name is Spade. Now all four of you are going to bet that the top card off the deck will be a spade.

If you have the idea by now, then you know that the odds of any card being a spade are one out of four, or 3 to 1. And that's what we have set up here; three players against one. Put a chip from each player in the pot and turn the top card off the deck. If it's a spade, then you win the pot, if it's a club, then the club player wins the pot and so on. Repeat this until the deck is gone. Who has how many chips? Every player will have exactly as many as he started out with. You are making a bet where the odds of winning are 3 to 1 and those are the exact odds you are being paid. Your expectation in the long run is zero.

Negative Expectation Example

Now we will look at negative expectation. Divide the poker chips into three equal stacks instead of four. You are playing against two other players instead of three. This means that you are now getting 2 to 1 on your bets instead of 3 to 1. Perform the above exercise again and award the pots to the Club and Diamond players until all of the cards in the deck are used up. Whenever the Heart player wins, you can divide his pot in two and give it to the two other players since he is not in the game. Of course, you still win the spade pots.

Now what happened? Since there are still thirteen spades in the deck and you won thirteen hands just as you did in the zero expectation exercise, your chances of winning obviously did not change. What changed, however, were the odds you were being paid to draw to your hand. This is why, when you are drawing to a poker hand that has a 3 to 1 chance of being completed, you need to be assured that the pot is offering you odds of at least 3 to 1 when you do make the hand.

Let's look at an example of negative expectation as it happens in an actual hold'em game. Give yourself 5♠ 2♠, put A♠ K♠ J♦ up as the flop, and the 10♥ as the turn card. Divide your chips into two equal stacks and give your sole opponent Q♦ 9♥. He already has the nut straight on the turn and clearly your only out is to make your spade flush. Here goes. Put one chip in the pot from each stack and turn the top card on the deck. Award the pot to the winner and keep repeating this until all the cards in the deck have been used.

What happened?

You beat his straight nine times with a flush. You made the hand you were hoping to make, and yet you still lost money. The pot odds were obviously not correct for you to draw to a flush.

The real-life practical lesson you should learn from this is the following: Don't draw to a flush heads-up if making the flush is your only out. As you have just proven to yourself, it's a losing proposition, even though you will make the flush nine out of forty-four times.

Positive Expectation Example

Sticking with the same example, since we are so familiar with it, let's take a look at how positive expectation works. Recognizing positive expectation situations and betting opportunities is the backbone of being a winning poker player, regardless of the specific type of poker you are playing.

This time, divide your chips into two stacks, one with ten chips and the other with all the other chips you have. The ten-chip stack is yours and the other stack represents the six other players in the hand with you. Set up your flush draw as in the above example. Put one chip in the pot from your stack and put six chips in the pot from the other stack since there are six opponents playing against you. You can divide your opponent's stack into six smaller stacks if it helps you see the example more clearly, but it makes no difference.

Play the deck all the way down again and you'll see that your stack of chips will steadily grow larger and larger. This is because you are being paid better than 3 to 1 on a 3 to 1 draw. In fact, you're being paid 6 to 1 and now your draw to the flush has a positive expectation.

Positive Pot Odds

This also illustrates why it is usually correct to raise when you are on a draw to a hand and are getting pot odds that are much better than the drawing odds. To see this, try the exercise again using two and twelve chips instead of one and six. You win twice as many chips when the flush is made, but you lose only one extra chip when you miss. When you raise in this situation, you have to be reasonably sure that you'll win the hand if you do make your draw. The money in the pot that you win in this situation has to be enough to make up for the times that you miss the hand completely, and the times that you make the hand but still lose the pot.

You should always have an idea of how much money is in the pot at all times if you are in the hand. Get in the habit of keeping a cumulative total of the pot in your mind as bets are being made. Most of the decisions you will make in this game are automatic and it will not affect the quality of your play to mentally keep a side count of the pot size. I have found that it is easier to count the number of bets in the pot rather than the actual amount of money.

This is what I do: Before the flop, and on the flop, I mentally count, "One, two, three, four," etc., as each bet goes into the pot. A raise counts as two bets, because that's what it is. I continue the count on the flop. After all the betting is complete on the flop and the turn card is about to be turned, I divide my running count in half since the bets double on the turn. This way I always know how many bets are in the pot when I have to divide my bets into the pot size to get the pot odds.

BAD BEATS

There's not much more I can say about **bad beats**, statistically improbable draws, that hasn't already been said. Just keep in mind that you want your opponents to make these bad percentage plays. Here are a few things to keep in mind if you've suffered more than your share of bad beats:

- Don't give up your game plan. Stick to your basic strategy. Don't abandon those qualities that make you a good player.

- Don't give in to the temptation to play more hands in an effort to get even quickly. Remember, you're playing for the long run and you should understand that bad beats are a necessary part of the game.

- Don't get mad or upset. Sometimes it seems as if the players putting the bad beats on you don't have the social skills necessary to stay out of a barroom brawl. Some of them are just plain obnoxious jerks. Don't get emotional even though you feel like you're being taunted. It can only affect your game in a negative way.

- Stay in the game for as long as you're a favorite to win. Time at the table is a sure cure for recovering from bad beats.

- Keeping that in mind, you shouldn't pass up an opportunity to move to an even better game. Don't stay in a bad game just because you feel you have to beat a certain player out of a certain amount of money.

- Take a break. Get up when it's your big blind and go do something else until it's your big blind again.

- Tighten up your preflop starting requirements for an hour or so. This means you'll be playing fewer hands than average, but you'll have much better than average starting hands when you do play. This will cut down your exposure to the number of bad beat possibilities.

- Use this time to study your opponents. Try to figure out what their starting requirements are for each position.

- Realize that it usually takes both the turn and the river for a player to put a bad beat on you. That means that he'll be putting a lot of money in the pot to see the river card and when he misses, which will be often, you'll win some pretty big pots.

- Get a seat change. If possible, sit to the immediate left of the bad beat artist. That way, he'll always have to act before you.

- Ask for a deck change or a new set up. It doesn't necessarily change your luck, but it will make you feel better and improve your attitude.

- Last, and maybe most importantly, be willing to accept a temporary loss if you have to. There'll always be another game and another chance to get your money back. It's just not worth losing your entire bankroll in an effort to get revenge on one player.

PLAYING THE RUSH

Fortunately, there is a flip side to bad beats and it's called a **rush**. It's when you can do no wrong. Every card you touch turns to gold. There are times when it doesn't matter what you play or how you play it, you'll win a big pot. Your seat gets hot and you win nearly every hand. Even hands that you throw away would have won if you had played them to the end. It's a perfectly normal and expected part of the game.

In a ten-handed game each player can expect to win 10 percent of the hands dealt in the long run. But that does not mean that the wins will be evenly spaced out so that the player in the one seat wins this hand, the player in the two seat wins the second hand, and so on. You will not win every 10th hand on schedule or as a matter of right.

Your odds of winning the next hand in a ten-handed game are 1 in 10. Your odds of winning the next two hands are 1 in 100 (1/10 x 1/10). Your odds of winning the next three hands are 1 in 1,000 and the odds of winning the next four consecutive hands are 1 in 10,000. This, of course, assumes that all ten players play each hand against you, which is pretty unrealistic, even in a very loose low-limit game.

If only five players play against you, then your odds of winning one, two, three and four consecutive hands are 1/5, 1/25, 1/125, 1/625, respectively. So you can see how difficult it is to maintain a rush even under the best of conditions.

The problem comes in knowing when to stop pushing your luck when you're on a rush. There is no sure way to know, but I recommend that you go back to your regular degree of aggressiveness after you've lost two or three hands in a row. If you've lost two hands in a row, then one of two things is true:

1. Either you're still on the rush and your two losses don't mean anything, or

2. Your rush is over.

Considering how difficult it is to maintain a rush, and how seldom you do get a rush, it's easy to conclude that it's much more likely that the rush is over. Don't play purely garbage hands if the only reason is to keep a rush going. It just doesn't win in the long run. A rush can only be seen with hindsight, after the fact. But that doesn't mean you can't enjoy it when it's happening to you.

Realize that it's not necessarily folding, checking, calling, betting, or raising in itself that makes you a winner at this game. What makes you a winner in poker is understanding *why* you do what you do. Every time you have to make a decision in this game, you are trying to accomplish a particular goal. It's knowing what your goal is that tells you how to play the hand. For example, if you have the nuts, then you would like to get in a check-raise to make everyone call a double bet, if possible.

It's not the check-raise that makes you a winner, it's knowing that a check-raise is called for that makes you a winner.

Be aware that the later it gets, both in terms of how long the game has been in progress, and how late it is on the clock, the more mistakes your opponents will start to make, especially in a typical low-limit game. An expert makes his money by waiting for his opponents to get tired of playing correctly. An expert puts his money in the pot only when he is a favorite to win the most money in the long run. Your job is to strive to be that expert.

TIPS ON VARYING YOUR PLAY

If one out of every four cards in the deck is a heart, it does not mean that every fourth card will be a heart. Likewise, it does not mean that every thirteenth card will be an ace or any other card you name. You can deal five consecutive hearts off the top of the deck and you can look through half the deck and not find a single ace.

One-half of all five-card hands will be a pair or better, but as everyone who has played five-card draw knows, you can be dealt twenty consecutive hands without getting so much as a pair.

In the long run, the cards will average out. But in the short run, anything can, and usually does, happen. How short is the short run? Look at it this way. There are exactly 19,600 different three-card flops possible. You may play 100 hands and not see a flop that you like. But you should realize that 100 flops out of a possible 19,600 is only 1/196th of the total flops possible. One hundred hands may seem like a lot, but it is really a small number in the larger scheme of things.

Cards can and do run in cycles. The theory of large numbers says so. If you experience a period where it seems like nothing but the low cards are winning the pots, then it is a perfectly legitimate strategy change to start playing low cards. For a while. This would be an excellent time to vary your play so that you don't get a reputation as strictly a high card player. It kills your action when everyone knows exactly what kind of cards you're probably holding. The trick is knowing when the cycle ends and low cards should not be played anymore. Playing low cards, such a 7♠ 6♦, 6♣ 5♣ and 6♥ 3♥ do win some pretty big pots, but you cannot play them consistently if you want to be a big winner at this game.

If you do choose to vary your play by playing a hand you ordinarily wouldn't, here are a few tips to keep in mind:

1. A Raise Preflop

With a preflop raise, especially from a good player, you should consider abandoning the hand and pick another hand to vary your play. The preflop raise means you are a big underdog to win the hand.

2. Pick Your Hand

Try to choose a hand when you are in late position and there are a lot of callers already in the pot. This gives you the best odds and you might even have a positive expectation after the flop. An example would be if you limped in on the button with 7♦ 6♣ and the flop was A♥ 5♦ 4♣.

3. Winning or Losing

Consider whether you are winning or losing. If you are losing, then you probably shouldn't risk your remaining chips on such a speculative hand. You should be more inclined to vary your play if you're winning and have respect at the table. Whether you are winning or losing is also a consideration when deciding to play passively or aggressively. You normally don't want to play more aggressively than your hand warrants if you don't have that many chips left in the game.

4. Ace on the Flop

Be careful if an ace comes on the flop and it doesn't help you, because in a low-limit game it probably has helped someone else, even if everyone checks on the flop. This is especially true if you're in a jackpot game.

5. If the Hand Turns Sour

Don't be embarrassed to give it up. Save your money for your really good hands.

6. Disguised Hand

When you do play a hand that you're not known for playing, you'll have a very well-disguised hand for a while. Remember, as the pot gets bigger and bigger, it is less important that you disguise your hand and it is more important that you maximize your profit in the hand, even if you have to play the hand in such a way that you think might be giving it away. It's okay. By the time you get to the river and the pot is very big, your remaining opponents will either have the right odds to play or *they* won't. There's nothing you can do about it except make them pay to beat you, or fold your hand on the river and save a bet if it's obvious the river card beat you.

The concept of zero expectation has an important influence on your decisions to vary your play. Since you're going to win nothing and lose nothing in the long run anyway, you have great latitude in how you choose to play the hand. A good example would be if you have an open-end straight draw after the flop in which your odds of completing the hand are 2-1 and the pot odds are exactly 2-1.

Whether you fold, check, call or raise does not matter because you have zero expectation in the long run. If you're winning, then you can bet and raise to take advantage of your winning image. If you're losing, then you can check or fold to save money. And since you have zero expectation, you're free to play the hand in a completely different way than you normally do.

An excellent strategy would be to check-raise with the straight draw and then show everyone the hand, whether you make the straight or not. And then the next time you check-raise, you will have sown the seeds of doubt about your hand in your opponents' minds. They won't be sure of what you might have, and that, as they say, is the name of the game.

If you are losing and thinking about changing up your play, then there is one other thing to think about. If you have only $25 in poker chips and you have to call a $4 bet, then that $4 represents 16 percent of your total stake. If you have $100, then you're risking only 4 percent of your stake. Obviously, the loss of $4 when you have $100 is not nearly as bad as losing $4 when you have only $25. Even though the pot odds and the drawing odds may be the same in both instances, you should be aware that a loss is more devastating to you when you're losing and low on chips.

STRAIGHT LIMIT POKER

Straight limit poker is a game in which the allowable betting limits do not change at any time during the game. The most common examples of straight limit hold'em are $1-$4 and $1-$5 limit as opposed to a structured $3/$6 or $10/$20 type game. In a $1-$5 game, you can bet $1, $2, $3, $4 or $5 at any time during the hand. It's not a very common betting structure any more but you may still find games with this structure.

Here's a list of the most important things you'll need to know about straight limit:

- Players who buy-in for the minimum (usually $20) intend to play very carefully. When you see this player play his first hand, you'll know it's a much better than average hand.

- It's easier to save money if you're running bad or not catching any cards to play. Since there's only a single $1 blind, you can be very patient. The blinds will cost only about $40 in an eight-hour session.

- It's less expensive if you're playing speculative hands. You can see the flop for only $1 and fold quite a few times and still be able to make your lost blinds in only one hand.

- Because so many players will see the flop for only $1, you'll win a good-sized pot when you win the hand.

- The flip side to this is that you'll suffer a lot of bad beats because, as the pot gets bigger and bigger, you will only be able to bet $5 to protect your hand. The other players will often have the correct odds to draw to hands that they could not play if the bet doubled on the turn. Players are more likely, not less likely, to call when you bet on the turn and river.

- You will have more check-raising opportunities on the flop because you don't have to wait for the bet to double on the turn. There is no need to wait for the turn to check-raise.

- There are no free cards to buy since the bet does not double on the turn. Raising on the flop to save a bet on the turn doesn't work because it costs just as much to raise on the flop as it does to bet on the turn. That's not true in either the $3/$6 type limit games or a $1-$4-$8-$8 game, where it costs only $4 to raise on the flop, but $8 to bet on the turn.

- You'll probably have big swings in your bankroll in a straight limit game. That's due to the preponderance of weaker players who play every hand and who frequent these low-limit games.

There is one important lesson to be learned from straight limit that applies to $1-$4-$8-$8 limit. If you're going to bet or raise, then you should bet or raise the limit. Make them pay to beat you. If you bet $1 or $2 on the turn or river when you could have bet $8, then you are giving your opponents incredibly good odds to call and possibly beat you.

For example, if you bet $2 into a $40 pot, then the first player to call you is getting 20-1 on his money and that makes it correct for him to call with just about any hand he could have in a hold'em game. If he has an inside straight draw, then his odds of making the hand with one card to come are 11-1. If you bet $8 then he will have to throw his hand away because now he's getting only 6-1 pot odds on his 11-1 draw.

When you decide how much to bet, you are, to some extent, deciding what odds to offer your opponent.

PLAYING THE OVERS

Playing the overs is what you are doing when you are playing for a higher limit than that officially posted for the game. It is a game within a game.

Here's how it works: Assume you're in a ten-handed $1-$4-$8-$8 game and there are two other players beside yourself who would like to play higher limit. They're in the one and five seats and you're in the ten seat and you have an agreement to play the overs with these players. As soon as the other players fold leaving only the *overs players*, the limit changes to pot-limit or whatever other limit you've all agreed to. However, as long as there is one other player in the hand who does not want to play the overs, the limit does not change.

If you are playing the overs, the floorman will give you

a button that says "Overs" or if they don't have buttons available, they will write the word "Overs" on a piece of paper and give it to you. You are supposed to keep your button or paper in front of you in plain sight for all the players to see at the *beginning* of the hand. This tells everyone that you are an overs player. If you change your mind about it, you should turn your button or piece of paper over to show the word "no." That will indicate that you are not an overs player.

There are several reasons why you would change your mind about playing the overs.

1. You might have lost most of your bankroll and want to protect what's left by not having to call pot-sized bets.

2. You might be the biggest winner in the game and you want to protect all those checks in front of you by not having to call a pot-sized bet.

3. The lineup you are facing might have changed and there are players in the game who are better than you.

4. You don't want to risk losing your entire stack in one or two hands.

If you do not want to play the overs and there are players in your game who are playing the overs, it will never affect you. The limit cannot change if you're in the hand. If you do play the overs—and you should because you're a winning poker player regardless of the limit—here are a few things you should know about it:

1. Play Tighter

You should play a little tighter than usual before the flop. It can be very expensive to draw to a hand that is not the nuts and then have someone bet the size of the pot on the river. Hands like Q♥ 8♥, K♣ 10♠, A♦ 9♠ are pretty good hands in low limit, but you can lose a lot of money when you make a queen-high flush, a pair of kings with a 10 kicker, or a pair of aces with a 9 kicker when someone bets the size of the pot.

2. Limit vs. Pot-limit

Remember that the hand you start out with in a limit game may be the hand you end up with in a pot-limit game. The starting requirements for pot-limit are so much more stringent because the cost of a mistake is so much more. It costs more to lose a hand at pot-limit poker.

3. Stay to the Left

If there are only two of you who want to play the overs, you should try to move to that player's immediate left without making it obvious why you're doing so. Now your opponent will always have to act before you; you'll always have position on him. Every time he checks to you he won't know if you're going to bet, and if you do bet, whether or not you have a hand or on a steal. Every time he bets in to you, he won't know if he's risking a pot-sized raise.

4. If You Have a Calling Hand

If you have a calling hand, but it's not that good, play your hand in such a way that you don't unnecessarily drive out a non-overs player. As long as there's at least one non-overs player in the hand, you won't have to call pot-sized bets to draw to your hand, and you won't be bluffed out by a big bet.

5. Play the Overs

You should encourage other players and poker room management to let you play the overs. Most low-limit players do not know about playing the overs and when they learn about it they usually like it.

PLAYING HIGHER LIMIT HOLD'EM

Sooner or later, if you're a good player, you'll want to play hold'em for a higher limit. Actually, graduating to $5/$10 or $10/$20 should be your ultimate goal. You should not be intimidated by the higher limit because only the size of the bets as they relate to one another is important in a poker game. If you bet one chip, then the other players will have to call or raise with only one chip.

Imagine that you are playing in a $2/$4 game with a $100 buy-in. The blinds are $1/$2 and it takes either $2 or $4 to bet, call and raise. Now imagine that you played for six hours and you cashed out $250, for a $150 win. Now imagine that the checks you have just been playing with are red instead of white and they are worth $5 each instead of just $1. That means you've been playing $10/$20 hold'em with a $500 buy-in instead of $2/$4 and you won $750 instead of $150.

You got the same cards, played the same hands, made the same bets, raises and calls, and lost and won the same pots. Only the value of the chips was different. The drawing odds and pot odds are the same regardless of the limit you are playing for. The poker chips have no value until you cash out. My advice is to play for the highest limit you can *comfortably* afford. It helps you play your best game and it gives you the best opportunity to win some real money. After all, that is why you're playing poker, isn't it?

If you're going to play higher limit hold'em, here are a few tips to help you with your first foray into the big game:

1. Playing with Regulars

Most of the players you'll play against in a $10/$20 game will be regulars in that game and they will try to intimidate you with the stakes. They will bet and raise in a more physically threatening manner (to you) and they will attempt to bluff you out if you show any hesitation or weakness in the play of your hand. You will face more raises on the turn since this makes you call $40, what they know is probably a very large amount of money to you if they've seen you play in smaller stakes games.

2. Buy-in

You should buy in for at least $300 in a $5/$10 game and at least $500 in a $10/$20 game. A $500 buy-in for a $10/$20 game is exactly the same thing as buying in for $100 in a $2/$4 game.

3. Playing Level

Often, the players in a $10/$20 game are not better players than you are. They just have enough money to play a higher limit and get more enjoyment from these higher stakes.

4. Play Tighter than Usual

Play tighter than usual until you get accustomed to the game. When in doubt, you should tend to fold more in the early going.

8

THE STRATEGY AND TACTICS OF HOLD'EM

CALLING BEFORE THE FLOP

Calling that first bet is the most important decision you'll make in hold'em. You'll have to make that decision as many as forty times per hour, and when you do decide to call, it will almost always cost you more money after that.

The cost of voluntarily calling the big blind when you don't have to adds up over the course of playing thousands and thousands of hands. It's something you should know how to do correctly because the penalty for making a bad decision here is so great. Remember that a $2 bet saved is worth just as much to you as any $2 you could win.

At the beginning of every hand you should remind yourself of the following winning principles:

1. You can't beat the odds in the long run.

2. You cannot play hands out of position.

3. You cannot call raises when you don't have the right odds.

4. You cannot play a drawing hand in a short-handed game.

111

5. You cannot call hoping to get lucky.

Keep in mind that when you choose to play a hand, it's really you against all of the other hands combined. It's almost as if a single player gets to play all of the other calling hands and at the end of the hand he gets to choose which one to make his hand with.

You have to consistently play only hands that have a reasonable chance of improving to the best hand at the end. This is a perfect illustration of why you shouldn't give free cards if you have a hand. With a lot of players in the hand, almost any card in the deck can hurt you.

Whether or not you should call preflop depends on several factors:

Your Position

This is your first and foremost consideration every time you're dealt two cards. Play tight in early position and play looser only as your position improves.

The seat to the immediate left of the big blind provides you with the biggest opportunity to save the most money in this game. Because of the possibility of a raise, these are the only hands you should play in this position: A♣ A♦, K♥ K♠, Q♦ Q♥, J♠ J♦, A♦ K♦, A♥ Q♥, A♠ J♠, A♣ 10♣, K♥ Q♥, K♣ J♣, A♦ K♥ and A♥ Q♣. Any other hand, even 10♦ 10♥, A♣ 9♣ or K♠ 10♠, are just not profitable in this position.

Strength of Your Hand

This goes with your position. How strong your hand is depends upon your position coupled with the strength of your cards. Be careful not to play cards too weak for your position and especially don't play garbage hands like 9♠ 5♦, K♥ 4♦ or 6♣ 2♥. Play only those hands that are clearly winners in the long run.

Whether It's a Loose or Tight Game

You should call with slightly more hands than usual in both a loose and a tight game. It is popularly believed that you should play tighter than usual in a tight game but that is incorrect.

Playing looser in a tight game gives you more opportunities to win more hands because the tight players will fold more often, thereby surrendering pots to you that you won't have to play to the end to win. In a loose game that won't happen as often.

Strength of the Opposition

Your profit in this game comes from the mistakes your opponents make. Naturally, if everyone in the game is a better hold'em player than you are, then they won't make too many mistakes when playing against you, but you'll make a lot of mistakes playing against them.

One of the things that goes into the make-up of a better player is his ability to disguise his hand and make you play incorrectly against him (because you misread his hand). In other words, better players know how to play against you but you're never sure how to play against them. Don't worry though, I'll show you how to disguise your hands and put doubt in the minds of your opponents.

Prior Bets and Raises

Normally, the first thing that a preflop raise tells you is that you're already beat at this point and you're a big underdog in the hand. Most low-limit players go ahead and call to see the flop. This is a big mistake because you're bucking the odds from the beginning and that's not the way to play winning hold'em.

Another reason that this is a mistake is that you'll often get a piece of the flop and be tempted to call because the pot is so big and you have a draw. Now you get to lose a small bet on the flop, a large bet on the turn and another large bet on the river—and that's if there are no raises in the hand—and all because you had to see the flop. If this is how you play, then you are a typical low-limit player and cannot be a winner in the long run.

Whether You're Winning or Losing

Theoretically, winning or losing should have no bearing on how you play your cards, but in reality it does. Think of your poker playing as one life-long game where only your cumulative wins or losses matters. How you're doing at any particular stage of the game is of no substantial consequence since you're playing for the long run.

But if you do not have the bankroll required to tolerate large negative swings in your short-term luck, a series of losing sessions could wipe you out and keep you from playing the game at all. In that case, you have to protect what you have while you're in the game by playing more carefully. The easiest way to do that is to not play drawing hands that normally require a big investment to find out if you've made the hand or not.

J♣ 10♦ is a good example of a hand that you would normally play, but you should muck it if you're on a short bankroll. Stick with hands that don't need much improvement to win, such as big pairs and two higher cards.

PLAYING EARLY POSITION

It's very important that you learn how to play in early position since that's the position in which you're most vulnerable to raises. You have the built-in disadvantage of having to act first on every round of betting. If you have a marginal (undecided) calling hand in early position, you should remember:

1. Your call improves the odds for potential callers behind you. It brings in drawing hands (and small pairs) that might otherwise not be getting the correct odds to call preflop. That extra one or two players in the hand often turns your hand from a winner into one that has a negative expectation.

2. You won't even know for yourself what kind of odds you'll be getting on your hand or how many players you'll be up against. This is why you have to play better than average hands in early position. You also don't know if you're going to have to play your hand for a double bet or not.

3. You can't play purely drawing hands up front. True, hands like K♦ Q♣ and Q♥ 10♥ are drawing hands but they can still win pots without making a straight or flush.

PLAYING LATE POSITION

Don't forget the one major inherent advantage that calling in late position has over calling in early position: The late position caller has much more information available to him with which to make his decision than the early position caller. If you're last to act, you're the most informed player in the game.

RAISING BEFORE THE FLOP

The number one thing that the average player can do to *immediately* improve his game is to quit routinely calling preflop raises unless he also has a genuine raising hand. This will have a big impact on your game because there's so much raising in the average low-limit game. In low limit, players will call with almost anything to see the flop. A raise means nothing to them. Realize that you're just building a pot when you raise preflop.

When you do raise, you should raise only with genuinely premium hands and not with hands that figure to already be beat before the flop. This is especially true when you're on the button and you raise. Very few players will throw away their hand when they know they have to call only one bet to see the flop.

A raise in early position will tend to narrow the field while a raise from late position just builds the pot.

One of the disadvantages of raising from early position is that you don't know who behind you would also liked to have raised, but only called. In other words, if you had only called, who behind you would have raised? Who wanted to raise but disguised his intention by just calling your raise? Some experts suggest that you should almost never raise preflop with any hand because you save more money in the long run that way. Since it seems that most flops are unfavorable, and if you raise you'll just get called anyway, you probably should see the flop as cheaply as possible most of the time.

However, everyone has a different level of understanding of the game. Hands like A-A, K-K and A-K, are going to be big winners for you in the long run regardless of how you play them before the flop. If you'd like to raise to build a pot because you know you're going to win more than your fair share of pots with these hands, then by all means do so. If you feel safer at this point in your poker education by just calling with these hands preflop , then that's alright, too. The point is that as your understanding of the odds and overall view of the game improves, you'll start to have more confidence in the certainty of long-term results and worry less about the results of any one particular hand.

If you are in late position and everyone has called and then you raise, you risk unleashing a raise from one of the players who originally called. This is a common situation in low-limit hold'em. Some players just like to build a pot and they figure that since it was raised anyway, they might just as well go ahead and reraise it. There are also a lot of players who like to raise in late position just because they are in late position and they know it will build a huge pot.

Sometimes you will be genuinely undecided about raising with your hand or just calling with it. You should ask yourself, "If my opponents could see my hand, would they prefer that I raise or just call with it?" Obviously, you should do the opposite of whatever they would rather have you do.

There are five major reasons to raise before the flop:

1. Eliminate Players

This is the most common reason to raise preflop. Most often you'll have a big pair or A♦ K♥ and want to narrow the field so your hand will have a better chance of standing up at the end.

2. To Get Value from Your Hand

You think you have the best hand and want to win as large a pot as possible. You will most often have a good hand in late position with many callers already in the hand.

3. To Gain Information

A player who raises preflop could have almost anything, but a reraise from you will help narrow his possible holdings. He could have anything when he raises, but if he reraises you, then he almost certainly has A♣ A♥ or K♠ K♦ in the pocket. If he had A♥ K♦ or a smaller pair, he would usually call.

You should know that three out of four preflop raising hands are *not* a pair. In other words, it is 3 to 1 that a preflop raiser does not have a pair. He almost always has two big cards and if an ace, king or queen does not come on the board, then he can usually be beat by any pair.

4. To Bluff or Semibluff

There are some pretty good players in this game despite the fact that there seems to be so many bad players. There are times when a raise or reraise from you just screams "A♥ A♦" and some players will throw their hand away right there or they'll call to see the flop and then fold it if they don't hit it perfectly. This gives you an opportunity to represent aces when you don't have them and it definitely puts your opponents on the defensive.

A lot of players would rather fold than pay to play a guessing game. Betting with a hand that is unlikely to win if called is a **bluff**. Betting with a hand that probably won't win if called, but has a chance to improve, is called **semibluffing**.

5. To Get a Free Card

It's very common for everyone to say, "Check to the raiser," on the flop. While you should resist this temptation to check to the raiser, you should train other players to check to you when possible. The advantage in having everyone check to you is that you can also check and see the turn card for free. Often, everyone will assume that you are now going to bet and they'll check to you again. If you want, you can check again and see the river card for free. See how one little preflop raise can enable you to see the entire hand for free?

If you're known to raise only with the best premium hands, then you're setting yourself up to have pots stolen from you. Players will always know what you have (or more importantly, what you don't have) and they will always know how to play against you based on the flop. That is why it is important that you occasionally vary your play and raise with different hands. Just make sure you raise with cards that still have a reasonable chance to make a good hand.

Raising with many different hands has the benefit of disguising your hand and getting calls from players who are misreading your hands. This works especially well when you raise preflop with two big flush cards and you make the flush. Most of your opponents will figure that you raised with a pair and couldn't possibly have the flush.

It's also nice when you raise with something like J♥ 10♣ and you get a flop like 9♠ 8♥ 7♦ or Q♦ 9♥ 2♣ and make the straight. Anyone who can beat A♦ A♠ or K♣ K♠ in the pocket will call you all the way down, just "knowing" he has you beat.

If there is a conservative player in your game, you will notice that he often does not even call the other $1 in the small blind to see the flop, even though there may not be a threat of a raise from the big blind. Keep an eye on this player. If he does call in the small blind, he probably has what you would consider to be a very good hand. He won't be loud about it or call attention to the fact that he's calling, but you should be aware of it. It's worth money to you. Play him a little tighter and more carefully than you would most other players. Also, a player like this is usually a very good player and you should give him credit for a hand when he's in the pot.

One important note about preflop raises: You should pay attention and remember who did the preflop raising. No one at the table, including the dealer, is allowed to tell you who did the preflop raising after the flop hits the board.

CALLING PREFLOP RAISES

It's important to know when to call a preflop raise and when not to. There is a big potential to lose a lot of money by becoming involved in a hand that you should not even be playing. When there is a preflop raise and you don't have any money in the pot, you need to evaluate your hand in a totally different way. You need a strategy for this situation. This is what you should consider:

Who Raised?

You have to know your players. Is the raise from a conservative, no-nonsense player? Or is it from the drunk who raises every hand? Is he an average player who just won a big pot? If so, he's probably playing a little too loose this time.

What Position is the Raiser In?

Is he in early position where a raise is clearly intended to drive you out of the hand? Or is he in late position where he knows you'll call since you already have one bet in the pot? Does he mind your call? A preflop raiser who makes you call two bets cold wants you out of the pot while the raiser who lets you call one bet and then another usually wants you to stay in the pot.

How Many Players Have Already Called?

Is there enough money in the pot to give you the correct odds to call? Did good players call from early positions, thereby indicating they have very good hands?

How Many Players Are Behind You?

The greater the number of players behind you yet to call, the better the pot odds will be to draw to your hand, and the more likely it is that you'll be reraised after you call. Take the time to look at the players on your left before you call. If one of them is thinking about raising, he'll often have enough chips in his hand to raise and you'll know that the betting will probably be capped before the flop. Remember that the raiser could have anything, but the callers really do have a hand. Can you beat both the raiser and the caller in this hand?

Who Might Reraise Behind You?

A reraise behind you cuts down on your pot odds, eliminates players, and reduces the size of the final pot.

How Big is the Preflop Pot?

Once the pot gets big in limit hold'em, it becomes "protected." That means that no matter what the flop, turn, and river cards are, or how the betting goes, the final bettor on the end will be called by someone, just because of the size of the pot. This means that you will have to have the best hand at the showdown. This rules out the possibility of bluffing on the end except on those rare occasions where everybody misses every straight and flush draw.

Are You on a Draw?

If you are on a draw, then you obviously need to improve your hand to win. If you have a big pair in the pocket, you are protected somewhat because you will still have at least a pair after the flop. Is your flush draw ace high? If not, this hand is going to cost a lot of money and you don't want to find out at the end that your K♥ 8♥ flush is beat by A♥ 5♥. Are you drawing dead? Are you holding A♠ J♣ against a possible A♥ K♦? You're a big underdog if you are.

Can You Beat the Raiser at this Point?

This is an excellent test question and it will save you a lot of money in the long run. The best hand at the beginning is usually the best hand at the end.

Ask yourself, "If I compare my hand with the raiser's hand right now, who will have the best hand? If it were a two-card contest, who would win?"

If he has a big pocket pair and you have a smaller pocket pair, you are an underdog. If he has any card higher than either of yours, you are not a favorite. On the other hand, if he has A♥ K♠ against your 2♦ 2♣, you are a slight favorite if you play all the way to the end. If he has A♣ K♥ against your A♦ A♥ or K♠ K♦, you are a heavy favorite and your reraise would tell him that.

When a player raises before the flop, the first hand you should put him on is A♥ K♦, and then A♣ A♦ and K♥ K♠,

. order. He may actually have something else, but this ᴠnat you should start with. You will just have to know ur player to know if he might have something weird or a non-standard raising hand. You should not put him on one definite hand and play it like that until the end. Instead, you should put him on a variety of possible hands and then reduce the possibilities from there by the way he bets and plays the hand.

A player who raises before the flop and then checks when there are no high cards on the flop almost always has A♠ K♥, A♦ Q♥ or K♦ Q♣. This makes his hand very easy to read and you'll always know how to play. A bet on the turn will usually win the pot for you if it's not a big card. This is why you should normally bet on the flop if you raised before the flop. It helps disguise your hand and it perfectly represents a holding of A♦ A♥, K♠ K♣ or Q♦ Q♣. An opponent would be hard pressed to call you on the flop unless he made a hand or a draw that in his mind could beat a big pocket pair.

A lot of low-limit players who call three or four bets before the flop become psychologically committed to defending their hands to the death. Or at least to the end. They will go farther with their hand than its value warrants. When the pot is very large before the flop, at least one player will have the correct odds to call to see the turn card, which builds the pot, which in turn gives him the correct odds to see the river card. Expect to be beat once in a while by longshot draws when there is a lot of preflop raising and many callers.

If a preflop raiser checks to you on the flop and turn, you should bet into him with just about anything on the river, unless you think the river card somehow hurt you. I would check if the river card is an ace or king in this situation because you don't stand to gain that much by betting. Many players will raise preflop with A♦ K♠ in the pocket, flop nothing and check it to you when they make a pair of aces or kings on the river. If there is a third or fourth player in at the river, then you should be aware that an ace on the river probably made someone aces-up.

A player who exercises his option by raising himself while in one of the blinds will usually have a pretty good hand. The reasons are:

1. He knows he'll be in a terrible position throughout the entire hand since he's in early position.

2. He knows he'll be called.

3. He knows that he gave away the strength of his hand voluntarily, yet he thought it was worth it to get more money in the pot.

A player doesn't raise in this situation unless he expects to win the pot. Give him credit.

You can often steal a pot from a preflop raiser, even if he has a big pair in the pocket, especially if he's a good player. If it's just you and the raiser heads-up, and the board pairs on the turn, you can represent trips, whether you actually have them or not. You can either bet into him if you're first and have been checking and calling up until now, or you can check-raise on the turn. Obviously, if he's first and bets into you, you should raise without hesitation. If he has A♠ K♦, he'll have to throw it away without seeing the river.

The good part about this play is that many players will give you credit for the trips and throw away a big overpair. Sometimes an opponent will read you correctly for the steal and call your raise. If he *really* reads you correctly, he'll reraise with nothing in an attempt to represent aces in the pocket. That is why you should play it exactly like this when you actually do have the trips. You will get paid off for your better hand. And the next time you try it, he won't be sure of what you have because you've shown him that you're capable of check-raising with trips and with nothing.

When you reraise a raiser preflop, you usually get credit for having at least one ace in the pocket. If there's an ace on the flop and it's checked to you, you should definitely bet against only one opponent. Your opponent will throw away everything except A♣ A♥ and A♠ K♦. Since he knows you'll bet anyway, he will often check if he does have one of these hands. You have to be very careful if you're check-raised on the turn. It usually means you're facing a set and you're drawing dead.

Exactly how to play specific hands will be covered in a later chapter, but there is one hand that deserves special consideration while we're on the subject of calling preflop raises. That hand is K♥ 10♣, suited or not. You have a problem hand that could cost you a lot of money if there's a raise before the flop.

Compare your K♥ 10♣ to the possible raising hands:

- A♦ A♠ - You're already beat and you're a big underdog.

- K♣ K♠ - You're already beat and you need to make a straight or trip tens.

- Q♦ Q♣ - You need a king with no queen on board, then you have to call.

- J♠ J♣ - You need a king with no ace or jack, then you have to call.

- A♣ K♠ - You need a 10 with no ace or king; you can, however, make the nut straight with a board of Q-J-9-x-x (but no 10).

CHECKING AND/OR FOLDING ON THE FLOP

The flop is definitely the time to get away from your hand if you're going to. This is when the players who have big pairs in the pocket, overpairs and top pair with top kicker, bet and raise to make the draws pay and to protect their hands. Depending upon what your hand is and what the flop is, you should know exactly what the odds are of making your hand and how much money is in the pot.

Refer to the table of Drawing Odds From a Deck of 47 Unseen Cards in the "Hold'em Odds" chapter. It will tell you what your odds are for making your hand by the river. You will often have to check and fold on the flop if there's a bet. Here are some common situations that would necessitate a fold on the flop:

1. You Have Two Big Cards

You have two big cards such as A♥ K♠ and the flop is something like 8♣ 3♥ 5♦ and there is a bet. You should usually muck your hand. Using the same table as mentioned above, you see that you have six outs, which gives you only a 24.1 percent chance of hitting an ace or a king by the river. The problem is, an ace doesn't necessarily help you because it could likely make someone else aces-up. A king doesn't necessarily help because you can't be sure if it makes the best hand or not. You should fold and not chase the hand.

2. You Have a Big Pair

You have a big pair in the pocket and there is a uniform flop that does not give you a hand or a draw. For example, you have K♣ K♠ and the flop is J♥ 9♥ 8♥ and there are several callers. Let it go. Anyone holding just one card to the straight flush has a 45 percent chance of making a straight or a flush. This is not counting the fact that you could already be beat and are drawing dead.

3. You Raised Preflop

You raised preflop and you totally missed your draw. You might be able to run it through one or even two players, but if there are more than two players, you should check and fold. It's too likely that any flop would have helped one of the several callers.

4. You Have an Ace

When you have an ace with a mediocre kicker and an ace flops, let it go if there's any interest at all in the pot, especially from an early position. It's just too expensive to call all the way down just to find out that your kicker is no good. At best, you will have a split pot and even when you do occasionally hit your kicker, the hand will still not show a profit in the long run. It's difficult to flop a pair of aces and then throw it away, but it's a move that you should get accustomed to making with a bad kicker.

5. You Have a Small Pair

You have a small pair and you get no help on the flop. Since you have only two outs, the chance of making the hand by the river is only 8.4 percent. And this is not even considering the times you make your hand and still lose.

If you have 5♥ 5♠ and the flop is 8♣ 7♦ 6♠, you almost cannot win even if you make your hand. If you get a 9, it gives you a straight, but it's very likely that it made someone else a higher straight. If it's a 5, it makes you a set of fives, but it makes a possible straight for everybody else. If it's a 4, it makes you a straight and this is actually the best card you could hope for, even though you could still be beat. This type of hand just doesn't show a profit in the long run, especially if you play it against many players.

6. You Get a Nondescript Flop

You get a nondescript flop and the blind bets into a large field. He will often have flopped two pair and has to bet it to protect himself against the possibility of an overcard on the turn helping another player. The blind will ordinarily not bet if he has just a pair with a medium-strength kicker. He will have a much better hand than that. You should throw away most average hands in this situation. If you call, you're just playing a guessing game because a blind hand could have anything.

7. If You Are Check-Raised

You are check-raised on the flop and you have only an average hand. You will usually be beat at that point and the check-raiser is trying to build a pot and he knows you'll call. You should not call if you read him for a bona-fide hand.

Being able to throw away a hand when you only have to call one bet to see the next card is one of the hallmarks of a great player. It's difficult to do at first, but it's very profitable. One good way to figure out what to do is to ask yourself, "Does he expect me to call his check-raise?" If you feel that the answer is "Yes," then you should fold.

8. When the Flop Contains a Pair

You should consider folding when the flop contains a pair and you don't have one card of that rank. This is especially true when it's a big pair because of the likelihood that players call with the big cards. You should normally not draw to a straight or a flush when the flop has a pair. The chance that someone flopped trips, and the fact that you'll make your draw only 35 percent of the time, makes it a very expensive proposition. You could already be facing a full house on the flop and you could still lose even if you do make your draw.

Here's a good rule of thumb that will keep you out of trouble and save you a lot of money: When the flop contains a pair, you need to have one of the paired cards (to make trips), or an overpair to continue playing. Do not be lured into a false sense of security if a pair comes on the flop and no one bets. It would be correct for a player who flopped trips to check on the flop. He would be slowplaying the hand and giving everyone a free card to catch up with on the turn.

Checking with the intention of calling any bet is a very common situation on the flop. When you check on the flop, you should try to convey the impression that you have a hand, but you are opting to check anyway. If you instantly and enthusiastically check on the flop, and pick your cards up like they're two pieces of garbage, the other players will bet into you with anything, everything and nothing. You encourage bluffs when you make it obvious that you flopped nothing.

You should also be careful that you don't check out of turn. This indicates that you have a hand that you don't want to invest any money on and that fact will also induce bluffs against you. An opponent will now be encouraged to bet into you with a weaker hand than usual because he knows that there's a better than average chance that you won't call. This is costly because it deprives you of the opportunity to win a pot when both of you have a weak hand, but yours is slightly better.

The most common situation in which you would check and call is when you flop a straight or flush draw and you don't want to be raised if you bet. You would also check if you flopped a monster hand and wanted to slowplay it, or to give the impression that you don't have anything if you intend to check-raise on the turn.

Two out of three times that you flop a split pair, you will have second or third pair. For example, if the flop is J♠ 8♥ 5♦ and you're holding an 8 or a 5. Generally, if you wouldn't call with bottom pair, then you shouldn't call with second pair either. If another player has a jack with a good kicker (in this example), then it makes absolutely no difference if you call him down with an 8 or a 5. You have exactly the same chance of improving with either hand.

There is one slight advantage to calling with bottom pair, if you do call. That is, in hold'em, it is generally assumed that players don't play low cards, and if they do, they don't call, even if they flop bottom pair. So, it is usually considered to be a safe bet when the lowest card on the flop pairs on the turn or river. You will have a disguised set of trips and you'll usually win against a bigger two pair. You are definitely taking the worst of it when you play bottom pair unless you have something else going for you like a straight draw or a semibluff.

Calling with bottom pair and an ace kicker is a good semibluff. You know you don't have the best hand, but you know if you make an ace or trip your pair, you'll probably have a winner.

BETTING ON THE FLOP

If you see the flop and are genuinely undecided between checking and betting, you should usually choose to bet. Betting is better for these good reasons.

1. You don't give any free cards.

2. You won't get beat on the river by a player who would not have called if you had bet on the flop.

3. You give the drawing hands the worst possible odds to play their hands.

4. You could win the hand right there without a contest.

5. You will win a bigger pot if you do win the hand.

There are several specific times when you'd want to bet it right out on the flop if you're first to bet or it has been checked to you:

1. You Flopped a Good Hand

You don't want to give any free cards. You expect to win the hand if no one else improves. A good example would be if you have A♥ K♦ and the flop is K♣ 8♠ 3♥ against one or two players. You are a big favorite if the callers also have a king in the pocket.

2. You Raised Preflop

You're representing a big pair in the pocket. Even if you missed your hand, you will often have the best hand at this point and no one will want to pay to draw out on you. Even a player who flopped a weak pair with a bad kicker will usually throw his hand away.

3. You Think a Player on Your Left Will Raise

And you don't mind. You want the players behind him to call a raise cold because it helps protect your hand. You have K♥ 10♦ and the flop is K♠ J♣ 7♠. If you check, you risk giving a free card to the flush and straight draws. If you check and there's a bet, you can never be sure of what the bettor has. If you bet and there's a raise, you can be pretty sure that the raiser has a king and is trying to protect his hand. Players with flush draws usually don't raise in early position because it cuts their pot odds down and it drives their customers out.

4. You Flopped a Set of Aces

If you flop a set of aces, you want to bet, especially against many players. When you have two aces in the pocket and you get one more on the board, you will always be looking at a possible straight draw. Even if it's not probable, it's still possible. There's no way you can flop an ace and two different other cards and not have a straight draw. Try it. Because of this you will usually want to bet it right out and not give any free cards.

Even if nobody had the straight draw on the flop, the turn card might give someone one. This is especially true if the flop is an ace and two high cards and the turn is another big card. You would not have to worry as much, though, with a flop like A♦ 7♥ 2♣. Even though a straight draw is possible, it's not that likely.

If you flop a set of aces, you have to bet to protect them because the turn card could complete a straight draw or present a possible straight draw. You could flop a set of kings or queens and the other two cards on the flop could be something like 7-2 or 8-3 (no straight draw possible). With a flop like that, you often need to check to give them something to call with on the turn. If you flop a set of jacks, there's no way to have four other cards out there that don't make a straight possible if you don't fill up with a pair on the board.

If there was a lot of betting and raising before the flop, and you flop a good hand in late position with an ace or king on the board, you should be aware that it probably helped someone, whether there's a bet or not. It is more than likely that someone is going to check-raise if there's a bet. You should bet your good hands for value but you should also occasionally check with that same good hand to vary your play.

If you flop a good hand, your decision to bet or not depends on the strength of your hand, how many players are in the hand, the chances of getting an overcard on the turn or river, and of course, your estimation of what your opponents are holding. The more vulnerable you think your hand is, the more inclined you should be to bet to protect it.

There is a very good way to vary your play in this situation and that is to check and fold even though you have a hand that most players would consider to be reasonably decent. A good example would be holding J♦ 8♠ with a flop of J♣ 5♠ 4♦. Against a large field, I don't think you lose that much by checking and folding even though you have top pair on the board. Anyone else holding a jack most likely has you outkicked and there may even be a hidden overpair in the pocket out there.

RAISING ON THE FLOP

The first thing that you should know about raising on the flop is that it is not going to force out any player who flopped any kind of hand at all or any kind of flush or straight draw. No low-limit player is going to throw his hand away if he flopped a four flush, an open-end straight draw, an inside straight draw, a set, two split pair, top pair, an overpair, or if he has a pair in the pocket.

Many low-limit players will flop absolutely nothing and they will call to see the turn card just to see if they can pick up a straight or flush draw. For example, a player holds 8♦ 7♦ and the flop is A♦ 6♠ 2♥. He has absolutely nothing, but one of twenty-two cards will give him a straight or a flush to draw to—ten diamonds, three tens, three nines, three fives and three fours. This gives him an incredible 46.8 percent chance of picking up a draw on the turn even though he has nothing on the flop.

Using the table of Drawing Odds From a Deck of 47 Unseen Cards in the "Hold'em Odds" chapter, you can see that he then has a 19.6 percent chance of completing his flush and a 17.4 percent chance of making the straight draw. Even though this is a bad play, once he does pick up the draw on the turn, it's the same thing as if he had the draw on the flop but missed on the turn. The difference is that he will have to pay to see the turn without a draw if he wants to play like this and that's where you'll make your money.

Again, make opponents pay to draw out on you. All you're doing when you raise on the flop is building a pot, even though your intention is to give them the wrong odds to play. You'll just have to take your bad beats in stride, knowing that you will be a winner in the long run.

You Have Top Pair/Top Kicker

You should definitely raise and reraise if you flop top pair with top kicker and think you have the best hand at that point. You are a 2 to 1 favorite against any single straight or flush draw and a 4 to 1 favorite over any other player who has top pair with a weaker kicker than you do. Don't let opponents draw out on you for free. This is the most common reason you'll get called if you bet. There are other reasons (like your opponent holds a pocket pair), but these reasons are statistically less likely if you get called. You hold something like A♦ Q♥ and the flop is Q♠ 10♦ 5♣. You have top pair with top kicker and you're usually a favorite to win the hand.

A side benefit to playing your hand like this is that when there is also a flush draw on the board, your opponents won't know which of the two hands you have; the top pair or the flush draw. This little bit of doubt in their minds helps you because you'll be called slightly more often on the river when the flush card does not come.

If your opponent knew you flopped top pair, then he wouldn't have to call on the river if he knows he can't beat it. But, if he thinks you might have a flush draw and missed, and he can beat that, then he'll call you more often on the river. The possible flush draw raises the possibility that you missed and could be bluffing. And all of this just because of one little raise on the flop.

There is one situation in the above example that you should be wary of. That is when you flop top pair with top kicker and there is a bet, a raise, a reraise and another reraise, all on the flop. I want to tell you for a fact that you are positively beat at this point and you're probably drawing dead. It is very likely that someone flopped a set of queens, tens or fives, or someone has flopped two pair, queens and tens. There is also a good chance that someone has a pair of aces or kings in the pocket. And you have to be especially careful if one of the raisers is in the blind. He could have *anything*, got a miracle flop, and is now betting to protect it.

Look at it this way: For you to have the best hand at this point, your opponents would have to be doing all of this betting and raising with less than a pair of queens with an ace kicker. Ask yourself, "Would they be doing all of this betting and raising if they couldn't even beat a pair of queens with an ace kicker (or whatever your hand is)?"

If the answer is "No," then you should throw your hand away, even if you only have to call one more bet to see the next card.

You Suspect Your Opponent Missed the Flop

Another time to raise on the flop is if you suspect the preflop raiser has A-K and has missed on the flop, which will happen 73 percent of the time. One way to tell if he missed on the flop is if, in your mind, he bet it out too fast. If he actually did have pocket aces or kings, he'd have to take a second to look at the flop to figure out all the possible draws and how the flop affects his hand. But, since he's already decided he's going to bet regardless of what the flop is, he doesn't need any time to decide what to do, does he?

Since it's often correct for him to bet one time even when he misses, you would like to find out what he's got while the bets are still relatively cheap. A raise here will often win the pot outright if he does have the A-K. If you only call on the flop, you are giving him an uncontested chance to pick up an ace or king on the turn or river to possibly beat you.

Remember, three out of four times that a low-limit player raises preflop, he does *not* have a pair in the pocket. If you are reraised, you should probably give him credit for the overpair and muck your hand since it now appears that you are the underdog.

Getting a Free Card on the Draw

Another common reason to raise on the flop is to get a free card if you are on a draw. Actually, you are not really getting a free card. What you are getting is a cheap card. This is how it works. You are in late position with A♥ 8♥ and the flop is K♥ 7♥ 5♣. There is a bet from an early position and you get four callers. When it gets to you, you raise and everybody calls. From this point, the hand is going to turn out one of two ways, and they are both profitable for you:

1st Scenario

Your raise on the flop indicates that you have a good hand. Everyone gives in to the temptation to "check to the raiser" and that's what happens on the turn. The turn card does not help you and you also check. The river card is not a flush card (you missed your heart draw) and you don't call on the river if there's a bet. You got to see the turn and river card for free (actually it cost $4) and you did not have to pay to draw to your hand. Raising to get a free card saved you a total of $16 ($8 on both the turn and river). You got to draw two cards to the nut hand without having to pay for the privilege.

2nd Scenario

The turn card is a flush card. You now have a heart flush and the nuts at this point. You bet and get called on both the turn and the river. You win the hand and your raise on the flop got $4 more from four other players that would not have been in the pot if you hadn't raised. In other words, you got in an extra bet with a winning hand.

Whether you win the hand or not, your raise on the flop saves money if you miss your hand, and it makes you more money when you win the hand. It's a win-win situation. If you have trouble imagining this, try this simple exercise. Give yourself A♠ J♠ and put K♠ 8♠ 4♥ up as the flop.

Give yourself and four imaginary opponents thirty chips each for each of the following examples—1, 2, 3 and 4.

You're going to perform four exercises and write down on a piece of paper how many chips you are left with at the end of each one.

Exercise 1

Put $2 from each stack into the pot to represent everyone's call before the flop. You get the same flop as above and when it's your turn to call, you raise and everyone else calls. Now put $8 from each stack in the pot to represent this bet and raise with everyone calling. The turn card is not a flush card but you call the $8 bet along with everyone else. Put $8 in the pot from each player's stack. The river card is not a flush card and you have to fold. Award the pot to a player and record how many chips you have.

Exercise 2

Put two chips in the pot from each of the five stacks of chips. This represents everyone's call before the flop. Now you get the above flop and everyone calls $4. Put $4 from each stack into the pot. The turn card is not a spade but there is a bet and everyone calls. Put $8 from each stack into the pot. The river card is not a spade and you have to fold. Award the pot to any of the imaginary players you choose. Count the remainder of your chips and write that number on the piece of paper in front of you.

Exercise 3

Put $2 from each stack into the pot to represent everyone's call before the flop. You get two spades on the flop and when there's a bet, you just call. Put $4 from each stack into the pot. The turn card doesn't help but you call on the turn anyway. Put $8 in the pot from each stack. The river is the 2♠ and when it's checked around, you bet and everyone calls. You win the hand and enter the number of chips you now have on your paper.

Exercise 4

Put $2 from each stack in the pot to represent everyone's call before the flop. The flop has two flush cards and when it's your turn to call the bet, you raise and everyone calls. Put $8 in the pot from each stack. The turn card does not help you but everyone calls. Put $8 more in the pot from each stack. The river is 2♠ and you now have the nut flush. Everyone checks and calls when you bet. You win the pot and enter the number of chips you have.

Predictable Conclusion

Notice that you have more money in your stack with each succeeding exercise and that you save the most money when you raise and miss. And of course, you make the most money when you raise and make it.

As you can see, raising and missing is actually cheaper for you than just calling and missing. It's no big surprise that you make more money when you raise on the draw and make it. The surprise is that you save more money when you raise and miss. Try it, you'll like it.

Interpreting Raises

Players will raise on the flop for a variety of reasons but they will rarely raise when they flop a monster hand in a pot they really expect to win. Most typical low-limit players will wait for the turn, when the bets double, to raise or reraise. (This is not true of high-limit players.) They don't want to give away their hands on the flop for only one extra small bet. This is especially true when a preflop raiser just calls when an ace or king comes on the flop, but raises on the turn. This play strongly suggests that he has a set of aces or kings and slowplayed it on the flop.

For this reason, a player who does raise on the flop is less likely to end up with a full house. When he does raise on the flop, he usually will not have the two pair or trips that it takes to improve to a full house. An exception would be if the raiser was in the blind, in which case you'd better be prepared for any type of hand on the river.

Straight Draw versus Flush Draw

If there are many callers on the flop and you have a straight draw, you should usually not raise if there is a two-flush on the flop. Any player who flopped a four flush is not going to fold anyway because he knows he'll make the flush one time in three. You don't lose that much by just calling or even folding with a straight draw.

Flop Summary

The flop is when most players decide to either muck their hands or play to the river. A raise from you will help get out the undecided players and further reduce the number of players who see the turn to draw out on you. An extra $4 bet now could, and often will, win you the pot at the end.

PLAYING ON THE TURN

If you've decided to see the turn card, you probably know exactly what you need to win and what the odds of making it are. Chances are, you've also decided to see the river card in the event you missed your draw on the turn. If you have top pair or make two pair on the turn, you will usually bet and raise to protect your hand and to make the draws pay.

There are a few other miscellaneous things you need to know about playing on the turn:

1. Checking on the Turn

When you check on the turn, you are, in effect, giving your opponents not one, but two free cards. They can check with you and then get a look at the river card before they have to put any money into the pot. This really reduces your odds of winning the pot. There are many times when neither you nor your opponent has a decent hand but his is just slightly better. He may have a garbage hand that he wouldn't call for two cents, let alone $8 or more. But since you didn't bet, you are really forfeiting with the best hand. If you have anything at all, especially if a sole opponent checks to you, you should bet.

2. If You Are First

If you are first and are checking and calling because you're drawing to a straight or a flush, you should usually bet it out when you make the hand. That is, you should go ahead and bet into the player you previously checked to. It is critical that you play it this way for two important reasons:

> **a.** Now that you have the best hand you should make them pay to beat you. Getting second-best hands to pay you off when you have the winning hand is the essence of all forms of poker.

> **b.** If you check, you risk losing bets when you have the best hand and players check behind you. A good exception would be if you know, based on your experience and judgment, that the player on your left will bet and you can check-raise. We'll talk more about check-raising later in this chapter.

Another time to check when you make your hand on the turn, is when you think that by checking, a player will bet into you—but that player would not even call if you bet. In other words, you should check if you think it will induce a bluff from a player who would not call if you bet. There's more about bluffing later in this chapter, also.

3. A Player Who Has Bet Aggressively

A player who has bet aggressively before and on the flop, and then checks on the turn usually has one of these hands:

a. Two big overcards such as A♥ K♦. This is especially true if he's last and it's been checked to him.

b. An overpair but the turn card looks like it could have completed a straight or flush draw.

c. An overpair, but the turn card paired the highest card on the flop. For example the flop is J♠ 8♦ 3♥ and the turn is another jack. He might have been able to beat someone holding a jack but he can't win now because it looks like his opponent just made three jacks on the turn. He has nothing to gain by betting.

d. Top pair with a good kicker but it appears that someone else could have made two pair. For example, you have A♦ J♥, the flop is J♣ 8♠ 5♥, and the turn is Q♥. It is likely the Q♥ helped someone make either queens and jacks, or a straight.

e. An inside straight draw without the right pot odds to draw to it.

f. A pair in the pocket lower than the highest card on the flop. He bet it one time on the flop to represent top pair and is now checking.

4. Third High Card on the Turn

Most low-limit players will play any and every time they're dealt any two of the top five cards (ace through 10). If two of these cards come on the flop and a third comes on the turn, then it is extremely likely that someone has made a straight, or at the very worst, a one card draw to the straight. The chance of making a gutshot straight with one card to come is only 8.7 percent, so if that's the draw you put someone on, then you should make him pay to make it.

5. Here's a Tip

The following tip saves me a few dollars on the turn once in a while. If I'm in a $1-$4-$8-$8 game with a player who habitually makes string bets, I will usually not correct him. When it's obvious he intends to bet $8 on the turn, but only puts $4 out there and then goes back to his stack to get $4 more, I don't say anything if I intend to call anyway. But if I have a hand that I'm not too proud of and I want to see the river for as little as possible, I yell "Call" as soon as he puts that first $4 in the pot. According to the rules, he cannot bet any more than that unless he said he was going to before he put the $4 in the pot.

There's a variation of this play that will save you some change in the long run. If you're first on the turn and you have that same lousy hand, you can bet $4 instead of $8 if you don't fear a raise (and having to ultimately call an $8 raise in addition to your $4 bet).

6. Here is an Advanced Play

This move comes into play when you have an ace in the pocket. Assume you have the A♠, the flop has two spades, and a third spade comes on the turn. You can bet it right out as if you had the spade flush. After all, you're the only one who knows your other pocket card is not a spade. You will often win the pot right there, and if you do get called, you have a 19.6 percent chance of making the spade flush on the river. You also have an additional 6.5 percent chance of making an ace on the river to give you a 26.1 percent chance to win the hand.

What makes this a good play, is that you know that no other player can have the nut flush and this makes it more likely that an opponent won't call you with a spade draw when you bet. Also, there are a few players who will actually throw away a completed flush on the turn if it's bet and their flush is not that high. They know that if you have a spade in the pocket higher than either one of theirs, they could lose a big pot. You just have to know your opponents to get a feel for the correct play.

7. If You Are Going to Call on the River Anyway

If you are going to call on the river anyway, you should consider raising on the turn, especially if you have a medium strength hand with a chance of improving on the river. The logic is that since you're probably going to put two big bets into the pot anyway, you can put it all in on the turn and possibly win the pot right there. You will be giving the impression that you have a great hand and this sets up an opportunity to steal the pot on the river.

Because of your raise on the turn, players will now muck better than average hands on the river. If you improve on the river, then you will have extracted an extra bet from the other players when you had the best hand. If everyone checks on the river because of your raise, then the play didn't cost any extra chips since it would have went bet-bet on the turn and river anyway.

In summary, the turn is when you have the first big opportunity to bet more, raise when the bets have doubled, and make the draws pay to beat you.

POT ODDS AND CALLING ON THE RIVER

The first thing you need to understand when it comes to calling on the end, is what your pot odds are. For example, if you're getting pot odds of 10 to 1 and think your odds of winning if you call are better than that, then you should call. If you think your odds of winning the hand if you call are less than 10 to 1, then you should not call.

Here is why this logic works: Assume that your chances

of winning the hand in the above example are exactly 10 to 1. You will call $8 ten times for a total loss of $80. This is the "10" in the 10 to 1 odds. Then you will call one time and win for a total gain of $80 (the $88 pot minus your $8 call). This is the "1" in the 10 to 1 odds. Your net win/loss after these eleven plays (10 losses and 1 win) is exactly zero. Since your odds of winning the hand are exactly equal to the pot odds, you have a zero expectation in the long run. And since you do have a zero expectation, it makes no difference if you fold or call in these situations.

Notice that if you win two hands out of eleven instead of only one, you would be ahead $80 instead of even. So, to justify calling, you have to have a better than 1 out of 11 chance of winning the hand. Whether or not you actually have those odds is up to your judgment and experience. When it's up to you to call on the end, all you have to do is divide the size of the call by the size of the pot. This will give you a number that we will call "X." Then you ask yourself, "Do I have at least a one out of "X" chance of winning this pot if I call this bet?" If the answer is "Yes," then you should call the bet.

This often leads to what sometimes appears to be some really silly betting and calling on the end, especially if the pot is huge and there are only two players.

Let's say the pot has $160 in it and the first player bets in to the only other player. The first player flopped the nut flush draw and missed. He knows that he cannot check and win and that his only chance of winning the hand is to bet and not get called. Since $8 goes into $160 twenty times, he needs only a one in twenty chance to win the hand to show a profit in the long run.

Now the caller, who also has nothing but can beat a pure bluff, only has to call $8 in to a $168 pot and have a one in twenty-one chance to win the hand. If he puts the better on a busted flush and knows that the bettor cannot check and win, (which is more often than one time in twenty-one) then he should call every time.

On the river, you have an opportunity to make a certain type of mistake that you usually don't get until the river. When it comes to calling a bet, especially on the river, there are two types of mistakes you can make:

1. A mistake that will cost you a single bet.

2. A mistake that will cost you the pot.

Obviously, the bigger the pot is, the more costly a mistake if you fold but should have called.

There is one other consideration when the pot is very large. That is: When the bettor is sure you have at least a reasonable hand and that you will probably call no matter what he bets or what type of poker hand you have. The question is, "Does he *know* he's going to be called?" If so, it's much less likely that he's bluffing and you should use this information to reevaluate your actual chances of winning the hand.

No pot is so big that you have to call if you are certain that you are beat. There are times, which you will learn from experience, when you just know that you are beat and you don't have to call that one last bet.

Here are a few miscellaneous thoughts about calling on the end:

1. Be Aware of the Pot Odds

Couple this information with who it is that is doing the betting. If you are getting terrible odds, for example, you have to call an $8 bet into a $24 pot and the bettor is a very good player, then you can usually fold the hand without much worry. On the other hand, if it's a $140 pot and it's just you and the loosest player in the game, I'd call his bet just about every time. Don't forget to consider the bettor's position and your estimation of what you think his hand is.

2. Having the Nuts on the River

Realize that if you make the nuts on the river and you have to call a bet in early position, you just might make more money in the long run if you call, rather than raise. It is better to have five players call behind you than to raise and get only one or no callers. Also, if you just call, there is a chance for someone behind you to raise, and then you can reraise.

3. Did the Draw Get There?

One good method of helping you figure out what the bettor might have when he bets on the river, is to compare the river card to the flop and see if it helps make a straight, flush or even aces-up. This is especially helpful when two to a suit came on the flop and the bettor checked and called until another card of that suit came on the river.

Another good example would be if the flop was Q♦ 10♠ 6♣ and an opponent checked and called on the flop, and again checked and called when the turn card was a 5♥. If the river is a king or an 8 and he bets it right out into you, then you can be pretty sure he's holding J♠ 9♦ and he made the straight.

4. You Make a Flush with Big Cards

If you make a flush with big cards, then you would like to make it on the turn so that weaker hands will pay you off in an effort to draw out on you. Anyone with a set has a 21.7 percent chance of making a full house with one card to come and anyone holding two split pair has only an 8.7 percent chance of making the full house to beat you. Make them pay since you're going to win the hand most of the time.

If you make a flush using small cards, like 5♥ 4♥, then you would like to make the flush on the river. This gives you the best chance of winning the hand because a player holding a higher heart in the pocket does not get any more cards to draw out on you. If you make your 5-high flush on the turn, you will lose to a higher flush 19.6 percent of the time. Do not slowplay either of these types of flushes since you either lose money when you have the best hand in one instance or you give a free card that could hurt you in another.

5. Don't Check, Bet

If you're going to check and call on the end anyway, you should consider going ahead and being the bettor yourself. If you check, you might induce a bluff from a player who wouldn't call if you bet. This is especially true when you're heads-up with just one player and the river was not a straight or a flush card. This also gains you a bet when you have a mediocre hand but your opponent calls with just a slightly worse hand. The added possibility that you could be bluffing will also get some calls on the end.

6. Flash One of Your Cards

Often you will have the nuts when it's just you and one other player on the end. If you bet and that player is genuinely undecided about calling your bet, you can show him just one of your cards to make him think about your hand. Usually, showing him one of your cards will pique his interest and he'll often go ahead and call just to see your other card.

If he decides to fold without calling your bet, it's important that you do not show your other card to him, or to anyone else for that matter. Why should he call your bet if he knows you're going to show the card after the hand anyway? And if you show it to another player or a spectator, he has the right to ask to see it also.

BETTING ON THE RIVER

There are two main reasons to bet on the river when all the cards are out and you are first to bet. The first is to induce a weaker hand to put more money into a pot that you think you are going to win. The other reason is to get a better hand to fold when you have the second-best hand. (You can also make a bet as a pure bluff when you have absolutely nothing—that will be covered in a later section.)

Betting on the end with the best hand is called **betting for value** and it will probably be the most common reason that you will bet on the end.

There is a two-part question that you have to ask yourself before you bet for value on the end and the answer to both of those questions has to be "Yes." That question is: "Does my opponent have a worse hand than I do and will he call with it?"

If his hand is better than yours, then you lose a bet and a pot when he calls. If he has a worse hand than yours, but he would not call if you bet, then you have risked a bet for a pot that you were going to win anyway. You also risk a raise if you've misread his hand, and you lose a bet and the pot because you'll have to fold.

You can see that you win the most when he has a hand worse than yours and he calls your bet with it. If the answer to either part of your two-part question is "No," then you should usually check.

Another time to bet on the river is when you missed your straight or flush draw and feel that your opponent did also, but holds two big cards. You feel that if you check and show that hand down, your A♥ J♦ will lose to his A♠ Q♣. You should consider betting in these situations because your opponent will be hard pressed to call you with only ace-high.

There will also be a few times when he will have made a pair but will not call with it. This is not the same as bluffing because in Texas hold'em, two big cards is often a good, legitimate hand at the end. Sometimes, because of the community card nature of Texas hold'em, A♦ K♣ is the best hand at the showdown.

There is another time to bet on the river, and the reason

is unique to Texas hold'em. Often the flop will not help anyone and opponents will check it to you. When the turn card doesn't help anyone it will be checked around again. When it is checked to you two or three times, your opponents are, in effect, telling you to bet it so they can fold and get on to the next hand. They have only a big blind in the hand and they're willing to let it go to get on with the game.

Afraid-You-Won't-Bet Bet

There is another situation to be aware of when it comes to betting on the river, and it's what I call an "Afraid-You-Won't-Bet" bet. Here is the way a typical hand will go in this situation. There is a bet and raises on the flop and a silent player just calls. On the turn, there is another bet and one or two raises and this same silent player still just calls. The river card comes and this silent player bets it right out, even though he's certain that someone else was probably going to bet anyway. He bet because in his mind there was a small chance it would be checked and he did not want that to happen.

This is how you should analyze the situation:

1. He has a great hand. Why else would he bet if he thought there was probably going to be a bet anyway?

2. He fully expects to win the hand and did not want to risk losing a bet, especially since he knows he's going to win the pot.

3. He doesn't care if his bet gives away the fact that he has a strong hand. He knows that there are other good hands out there that will have to call because of their strength. He also knows that, because of the previous action, there will probably be other callers just because of the pot odds.

4. He normally has exactly whatever it is he's representing, which is usually the nuts.

5. The last card did not hurt him, even if it appears to have completed the draws that his opponents might have been playing for. He doesn't care if they made their hands or not. He will often have the nut full house.

6. This play is often made by an older, conservative player in early position, and he doesn't care if it gives away his hand.

7. This is a very reliable tell in low-limit hold'em. Often the spectators in the hand will say something like, "Oops, another country heard from," or "It broke out in another spot."

If you keep track of the times that you see this situation occur, you'll see that you can usually throw away some very good hands without having to call that one last bet. Understanding and believing this will save you a lot of money over the years.

RAISING ON THE RIVER

There's not much to say about raising on the river except that you should almost always expect to win the hand when you do raise. Your raise cuts your pot odds in half for those bets that go in on the river. You are getting only even money for your raise. A couple of miscellaneous thoughts will close out this section:

1. I have never seen a check-raise bluff on the river in low-limit hold'em.

2. Don't raise with the smallest possible straight, flush or full house.

SPLIT POTS

Playing when you might possibly have a split pot is fairly simple and straightforward. The two main guidelines to keep in mind are:

1. Don't automatically assume that you have a split pot just because it's possible to have one.

2. You should always put in the maximum number of bets and raises any time you have the nuts, even if you think the pot might be split. You have absolutely nothing to lose if, on the river, you have the nuts and have the option of reraising a raiser.

You should also put in the maximum number of raises on the turn, even though you might be facing a draw to a better hand and the river card could beat you.

You will always be a favorite if you have the nuts on the turn and a single opponent has a draw to a better hand than yours. Referring to the table Drawing Odds From a Deck of 47 Unseen Cards in the "Hold'em Odds" chapter, you can see that a player drawing to a straight, flush or full house has only between an 8.7 percent and 21.7 percent chance of beating you with one card to come. You will usually be a favorite against two other players when you have the nuts with one card to come, but you should be careful when facing three or more opponents on the river.

You ordinarily would not want to play heads-up hands that could end in a split pot. There's no future in playing poker when all the money you can expect to get out of a pot is the money you put into it. The type of hand that frequently results in split pots is a big/little hand. That would be a hand like A♦ 3♥, K♠ 5♣ or Q♦ 4♣. This is because if you pair your big card, the rest of the hand will be completed by the board and your other pocket card will not come in to play. For example, you hold A♣ 2♦ and the board is A♥ K♠

10♦ 9♣ 7♦. Another player holding an ace with a bad kicker will split the pot with you.

It is actually a good play to muck your hand when you flop a pair of aces with a poor kicker, especially if you are facing many players and there is a lot of betting. The best you could hope for is a split pot and you will most likely lose the hand anyway.

Even though I have advised you to raise and reraise whenever you have the nuts, it seems that most low-limit players just call when it's apparent to them that they're going to split the pot. This is especially true when you're heads-up on the river and it takes only an ace in the pocket to split the pot. When you have the nuts against two or more opponents on the river you should definitely put in the maximum number of raises possible, and this is especially true if you have to use both of your hole cards to make your hand. It's very likely one of the other players will also have the nuts and you're "chopping up" the third player.

There is a problem hand here and it's when you have the nuts and a possible split pot on the turn, and the river card is a card that could beat you. For example, you hold A♦ Q♠ and the board is K♥ J♣ 5♦ 10♥, giving you the nut straight on the turn. You and a single opponent put in a bet and three reraises. The river card pairs the board, making a possible full house.

If your opponent is first and bets in to you, you should only call because you have nothing to gain by raising and his bet does not necessarily mean he has the full house. However, if you bet first and get raised, you are probably beat because players just do not raise on the end if they expect to split the pot anyway. Players see it as a waste of time and if they do raise you, it's because it's not a waste of time in their mind, which means you're beat.

CHECK-RAISING

You cannot check-raise all by yourself. All you can do is check with the *intention* of raising if there's a bet. So it follows that if you intend to check-raise then you should be very certain that a player close to your left will bet when you check.

There is often an objection to allowing check-raises in low-limit and home games but the objections are not logical. It's argued that checking and then raising is sneaky and underhanded because—now brace yourself—it disguises the strength of your hand and you are using an element of deception in a poker game. The objections always come from the weaker, less experienced poker players, and in my experience, players who want to play poker to win your money, but want a free ride from you when you have them beat.

The next time you get a complaint about your check-raise, you should ask the complainer, "How is it that I'm smart enough to know that you'll bet if I check, but you're not smart enough to figure out that I'm going to raise when you bet?" That usually ends the objections to check-raising right there. You should always want to play with check-raising because the more options that a good player has (that's you), the more money you can make at the game. Thankfully, the objections to allowing check-raising have all died out due to the exposure poker gets on television. Everyone now understands and accepts the fact that check-raising is an integral part of the game.

Interpreting an Opponent's Check-Raise

You would check-raise for most of the same reasons that you would raise, but because check-raising requires players to call two bets, it places an emphasis on getting more money into the pot and getting players out of the hand. A player who check-raises to make you call two bets cold usually wants you to fold, while a player who lets you call one bet and then raises you and other players, wants you to call. This is a big clue to the strength of his hand, especially if he could have made you call two bets cold but did not.

Strategic Check-Raising

If you have a great hand, you should be acutely aware of the position of any preflop raiser, if there was one. His position relative to you is critical in deciding whether or not to bet your hand right out or attempt to check-raise. If the raiser is on your immediate left then a bet from you will probably be raised and the other players will have to call two bets cold with the prospect of a reraise from you. If, however, the raiser is on your immediate right, then everyone will call when you bet and they will probably call again when the player on your right raises. Depending on your goal, you can use the position of the other raiser to help get other players out of the hand or help get more money in to the pot.

If there's a preflop raiser on your left, you should get into the habit of checking good hands to him on the flop and turn. You make more money by occasionally doing this. Since he raised before the flop, it looks natural for him to bet on the flop.

If you bet first, knowing that he's probably going to bet, then you have "cut off the raiser." This indicates that you have a super hand and kills your action. You won't get called as often because your bet is telling everyone that you can beat a raiser and that your hand is so good that you can't afford to miss a bet, even if it means giving away the strength of your hand.

Players will call the preflop raiser because it's expected that he'll bet no matter what comes on the flop. You should take advantage of this by checking your good hands to him on the turn and then raising after everybody has called his bet. You win more money because they think they're calling his hand and not yours. Obviously, if everyone knew that it is your hand they should be worried about, you would get a lot less action. Your check-raise disguised that fact and made you more money.

Will Your Opponent Bet After You Check?

If you want to check-raise, how do you know that a player on your left will bet if you check? Well, you can never know for sure, but there are a few factors that can help increase the likelihood that there will be a bet. The first consideration is the other player's position. The earlier the position he is in, the better the cards he should be holding. This makes it more likely that he'll bet on the flop. If he raised before the flop, then he is very likely holding good cards and he'll bet on the flop.

If he's a loose player, and especially if he's drinking, he's more likely than normal to bet on the flop. If he's just won the last two or three pots, he might bet just to see if he can keep his rush going.

A player who has a lot of chips is more likely to bet weak and marginal hands, which means that he'll be betting a lot more often than the strength of his hand warrants. You can check to this type of player more often.

High-limit players who are in a low-limit game like to bet much more often then they should. This is because they are accustomed to making moves and winning hands without a showdown as happens so often in a big limit game. Sometimes they feel they can bully low-limit players and feel they are too good for the limit they're currently playing. They don't give free cards (and neither should you), and they push their hands when they have small statistical advantages. For all of these reasons, you can count on them betting more often than the other players in the game. This, in turn, means that you can check with more confidence that they'll bet.

Taking the Flop Into Account

You also have to estimate how the flop might have helped a player on your left. A good example would be if the player on your left raised before the flop and the flop was K♦ Q♥ 3♣ and you held 3♥ 3♦. It is very likely that you can check-raise with your hand on the turn because of the K♦ and Q♥ on the flop, and the likelihood that it helped the preflop raiser.

Because of the fact that the bet doubles on the turn, a lot of low-limit players who make good hands on the flop wait for the turn to bet. It helps disguise their hands and it gets a lot more money into the pot since the bets are twice as large as before. Keeping in mind that the turn is when you should bet with almost anything—because this is where the garbage hands get out rather than call a large bet with a small pot—you should be wary when there are a lot of players but there is no bet.

Check-Raising by Position

The later you are in position and the more players there are who have checked it to you, the more likely it is that you are going to be check-raised. When this happens, and there is a bet on the river, you should be more cautious than usual about being check-raised and facing better than average hands. Very often, when there is no bet on the turn, it's because someone checked with the intention of raising but there was no bet to raise.

Check-raising on the turn is different than check-raising on the river because the check-raiser on the turn expects you to call his raise and then call another bet on the river. This means that he has a great hand and he does not fear the river cards beating him. You would be well on your way to becoming a great player if you could learn to throw your hand away in these situations and don't call the check-raise, even though you would only have to call one more bet to see the river card.

The check-raise has told you that you don't have the correct odds to draw even one more card. This is especially true when the pot is huge and the check-raiser knows that because of your position and the pot odds, you'd call anyway. One thing that you know for certain is that this is not a bluff. Disappoint him and get on to the next hand.

When You're Check-Raised
If you are check-raised and don't know what to do, remember that you know at least two things:

1. You know what your hand is,

2. You know that your opponent's hand is either better or worse than yours.

All you have to do is ask yourself, "Would he play his hand like this if it were worse than mine?" This is easier than trying to figure out exactly what poker hand he might have. Don't fall into the trap of trying to guess exactly what his hand is because you'll never know for sure and it often could be any one of many possible great hands. Which one it is doesn't really matter. Once you've determined that his hand couldn't possibly be worse than yours, that's all you need to know. As I said earlier, disappoint him and get on to the next hand.

Using the Check-Raise to Neutralize an Opponent's Edge
Sometimes you'll be in a game and over the course of a few hours the player on your left will, well, just beat the hell out of you. Every time you're in a pot with him he beats your brains out with the nuts or makes two pair with a 5 kicker to your two pair with a 4 kicker. Every time you check and call his bet, you lose. Every time you bet, he raises you and wins.

This is a common situation and it's just custom-made for check-raising. All you have to do is start checking your betting hands to him and raise when he bets. He'll be more likely to bet since he feels he has a psychological superiority over you and he'll be rudely surprised when he's check-raised. If it works, and you win the hand, you should do it one more time when you're certain you have the winner. This will make him have doubts about what a check from you really means, and fearing a check-raise, he'll start to check behind you.

What you have done is trained him to check to you. You won't have to call as many bets on the river when you have a marginal hand and you'll start to win more hands because you'll now be able to show down weaker hands without having to fold on the river. Many times both you and your nemesis on the left will have marginal hands and you'll show it down more often on the river without being bullied out of the pot.

Check-Raising with a Draw

Don't forget that you can also check-raise when you're on a draw. If the odds of making your hand are greater than the pot odds, then you'd like to have as much money in the pot as possible. You normally need many players in the hand to make it correct to check-raise on a draw, which is why you don't see this play very often.

Most low-limit players don't like to check-raise on a draw even when it is mathematically correct to do so. That is why you don't see this play that often in low-limit poker. This is also why, when you do decide to make this play, your hand will probably be well disguised if the flush or straight card comes on the river. Everyone will just "know" that the flush or straight card didn't help because you already had your hand when you check-raised on the turn. Because of the pot odds required, a check-raise with only a few players in the hand is not likely to indicate a draw.

Check-Raising a Set

You should not slowplay when you flop a low set (twos through eights) because of the possibility of being beat on the turn or someone picking up a draw that can beat you on the river. When possible, you should consider using the tactic of check-raising to protect your hand by making the other players call a double bet cold. Make them believe that an overpair in the pocket is no good, if you can. Often, it's worth winning the pot right there without a fight.

You should not be upset if you flop a small set and win a small pot on the flop. It's better than slowplaying your hand and losing a big pot. An exception would be if you're heads-up and the possibility of another card hurting you is not that great. But you should definitely bet it right out against a large field.

Hitting Perfect-Perfect

It's unlikely that you can hit perfect-perfect to make a great hand, so those times when you do, your hand will usually be very well disguised. The other players know this also and they will usually (and correctly) discount the possibility that it happened. Keep in mind that if you have to hit perfect-perfect to make a hand, it's because you probably had absolutely nothing on the flop.

The fact that you would call on the flop with nothing is really what disguises your hand. The other players will put you on several different hands on the flop and try to narrow it down from there, but one hand that they'll never put you on is "nothing." This makes a check-raise attempt more successful than usual.

Check-Raise or Bet?

There's a lot to say about check-raising but that does not mean that it is a big part of the game, especially in low limit. If you are in a hand and you are genuinely undecided about whether to check-raise or not, go ahead and bet your hand right out for value. You will definitely make more money by sticking to a simple, basic strategy rather than trying to get fancy. You should usually bet when you're strong and check when you're weak. Believe it or not, you make the most money this way and you do not necessarily give away your hands by playing them like that.

BLUFFING

This is the subject that, for some reason, excites everyone. I know that whenever I tell someone that I am a poker player, one of the first questions I get is, "Do you bluff a lot?" Yes, I do, but it's not that exciting and it's a common and ordinary occurrence in a low-limit hold'em game.

Bluffing in a limit hold'em game is usually a simple matter of mathematics coupled with an elementary understanding of how to read tells and figure out what your opponent's likely hole cards are. Because hold'em is pretty much an automatic game when it comes to decision-making, you will encounter certain situations over and over again.

Bluffing is a matter of mathematics because of the simple concept of pot odds. If there is $80 in the pot on the river and you bet $8 to try to steal that pot when you have nothing, then you are getting 10 to 1 on your money. Therefore, you need at least a 10 to 1 chance of winning the pot. If you bluff on the end ten times for a total investment of $80, then you need to succeed on the eleventh try in order to win back the money you invested on the other ten times you bluffed and failed.

As you can see, your bluff needs to succeed only a small percentage of the time for you to show a profit at bluffing. As a matter of fact, if you win the pot most of the time that you attempt a bluff, then you are not bluffing often enough!

Here's another way to look at it. Let's say that you just sat down in the game, flopped an open-end straight draw, and neither the turn or river cards helped you. You decide to try a bluff on the river and you bet $8 into an $80 pot, representing a good hand to the other players when in fact all you have is queen high. Two other players with better hands than yours fold and you win the pot without having to show your hand. You are now $80 ahead on attempted bluffs, and you've played only one hand.

If you mentally set that $80 aside and use it only for bluffing opportunities, you can see that you can attempt to bluff ten more times, and lose all ten of those hands, and still not be a loser when it comes to bluffing. One success in eleven tries is all it takes to break even in this scenario, and obviously anything better than one in eleven tries will show a big profit. Even if you win only two of eleven times you bluff, you will have a positive expectation.

It is wrong to have a policy of never bluffing in hold'em. Because of the community card aspect of the game, you will often be in a situation where you have only ace- or king-high at the river, and your opponent has only a slightly better hand, but it is a hand that he would not call a bet with. If you check, you lose when everyone gets to show their hand without having to call a bet on the river.

There are many times in hold'em when everyone misses their straight and flush draws and ends up with nothing, and all it takes is a bet to win the pot. Of course, you'll have to learn from experience when these times are, but they occur so frequently that it is worth your time and effort to recognize bluffing opportunities.

FAVORABLE TIMES TO BLUFF

There are no hard and fast rules regarding when to bluff and when not to, but there are some pretty good general guidelines to go by and there are a few specific situations that occur often enough to mention. Here they are, in approximately the order in which they occur in the play of the hand:

1. Because of the Pot Odds

It is correct to attempt a bluff more often when the pot is big, especially against only one or two players. In other words, the bigger the pot is, the more you should consider betting as a bluff if you missed your hand. As explained earlier, you do not need as big a chance of winning when the pot is smaller.

As an extreme example, assume that you have 5♥ 4♥ and the board is K♠ 10♥ 7♥ 6♣ 2♠. You flopped a flush draw, picked up an open-end straight draw on the turn and missed both draws on the river. There is $240 in the pot and your sole opponent checks to you. Obviously, if you check also, you lose. So you bet $8, knowing that you're getting 30 to 1 on your money ($8 x 30 = $240) and therefore, need only a 3.2 percent chance of not being called. In other words, if your opponent calls 96.8 percent of the time, you break even in the long run. If he calls less that 96.8 percent of the time, you make money in the long run.

2. Against Good Players

Good players are easier to bluff than poor players or your typical low-limit hold'em player. They're capable of putting you on a hand and giving you credit for it. Bad players will call you even when they know they're beat because they want to see one more card, or if there are no more cards to come, they'll call you because they can beat a bluff and nothing else.

3. When You Have A♦ K♥

When you have A♦ K♥, raised before the flop, and bet it out on the flop when you missed, you will often actually have the best hand at that point.

If you have A-K unsuited and miss on the flop, your success in stealing the pot without making a hand depends mostly on how many players you're facing and how much respect you have at the table. One opponent and a lot of respect, and you'll win just by reaching for your chips. Six opponents and no respect, you're just giving your money away if you bet.

4. When Your Strength Can't Be Read

You're the only one who knows for a fact at this point that you're bluffing. This gives you an incredible edge, because in the minds of the other players, you could theoretically have any one of 169 different hands, even though they may have you narrowed down to ten or twenty different hands. Since you will usually have the correct pot odds to bluff on the end, you have given your opponents another opportunity to make a mistake. Namely, you have given them an opportunity to make a mistake that will cost them the pot if they fold.

5. At Higher Stakes Games

Even though the actual stakes that you are playing for do not affect the pot odds, it seems that the higher the stakes are, the more successful an attempted bluff will be on the river. This is because as the stakes get higher, players fold progressively stronger hands without calling that final bet. A player who suspects you have A♣ K♥ and missed will usually call you on the river with 2♥ 2♠ when you bet $8. But he will fold more often when you bet $20 (in a $10/$20 game) and he has that same 2♥ 2♠.

6. Against Just One Opponent

You can usually run a cold bluff from beginning to end when you're up against a sole opponent who checks and calls all the way down. If you can give the impression that you have A♣ A♠, K♥ K♦, Q♦ Q♥ or A♣ K♣, you'll often catch a player who flopped a draw and will fold on the river when he misses. This works even when you "tell" him you have a big pair or he just "knows" it. Most average low-limit players will knowingly take the worst of the odds just because they "know" what it is that they have to beat.

162

7. When an Opponent Is Not Bluffing

When an opponent is not bluffing and he is certain you will call because of the pot odds or your position, he is usually not bluffing. These instances occur when the pot is huge, there are many players, or the bettor knows that it takes only one card to beat him. This is one time when you have to consider the action from the bettor's point of view. If he's first to bet into a $150 pot with five players, then he probably expects to be called and is not bluffing. On the other hand, if there's $20 in the pot and you are his only opponent, and you check and he bets, there is a greater than average chance that he's bluffing.

8. In Semibluff Situations

In hold'em the most common situation to semibluff is when you have A-X and you pair your X card. Usually you will have something like A♦ 8♦ and the flop is Q♣ 8♠ 5♦. You probably don't have the best hand but you can improve to the best hand. Another ace or 8 will give you a winner, in your opinion.

Your 20.4 percent chance of improving by the river, plus the fact that you can win by betting and not being called, all makes a bet with second or third pair and an ace kicker a very good proposition. You have so many ways to win the hand: you actually have the best hand, you can improve to a better hand, or you can bet and not be called.

Of course, there's a time when you should not attempt a semibluff. It's when there is a preflop raise and you flopped nothing or just a small pair. The preflop raise told you two things:

a. There are probably one or two aces out, even though you hold one.

b. You're a heavy underdog, also called **dog**, because you're facing a premium hand.

You have to make a good draw on the flop and then hit it to win the hand. There are only three other aces, and it looks like one of them is out. You also face the unpleasant event of hitting an ace on the flop, only to find out that someone has A♣ A♥ in the pocket.

9. Against a Bad Flop

Let's say that you're in late position, you get a garbage flop and you're sure that you have the best hand, even though it's not that high on the scale of poker hands. You're sure that a bet for value will win you the pot, but if you're called, you don't figure to have the best hand. It turns out that your bet was a bluff, but you didn't know it at the time. If you're going to continue with the bluff, it should be only if you're certain that the turn card did not give the caller a potential draw to call with. In other words, he could have flopped nothing, but picked up a straight or flush draw on the turn. This is a common situation in hold'em.

Most players who have called a bet and have two cards in their hand and four on the board will have at least a straight or a flush draw if they don't already have a pair. If, in your opinion, it's likely that the turn card made a draw for someone, you may not want to continue the bluff, especially if you're against more than one player. A good example would be if the flop had two high cards and the turn was another high card that also made two to a suit. Be careful if you intend to bluff.

10. Flop Pairs on the Turn With No Flop Bets

Another common flop that lends itself to bluffing is when there is a flop with no bet and the highest card on the flop pairs on the turn. Because of the fact that the top pair on the flop will be bet 95 percent of the time, you can usually be sure that the paired card on the turn did not make someone trips.

For example, the flop is J♠ 7♥ 3♦ and the turn is a J♣.

This is one of those rare times when you can bet knowing you're beat but won't be called. Anyone holding a 7 or a 3 will usually fold it, not wanting to risk the possibility that you have a jack and checked it on the flop. This player will consider the possibility that you were going to check-raise if there was no bet on the flop. As funny as it sounds, you can even show your A♣ K♥ to a player holding a 7 and he'll still throw it away, because of the pot odds.

11. Faking a Rush

After you've beat a certain player several times with the nuts, you should consider bluffing him on the river if you both get involved again. You've conditioned him to seeing the nuts from you and he'll give you considerably more respect than he would the other players. All you have to do is act like, "Here we go again," and he'll be more likely than usual to throw his hand away. After all, in his mind, you're on a rush against him. If everything is working for you and you're really lucky, he'll throw away much better hands against you than he would against the other players.

12. Stealing in the Blind Position

If there's not much interest in a hand and the pot is not that big for the limit you're playing, you can often steal the pot from one of the blind positions, even though you're in an early position. Your strength comes from the fact that you *are* in an early position. You obviously know it, and everyone else knows it, but you have chosen to bet anyway. Because you're in the blind, you could have anything, and that's just what you're representing.

UNFAVORABLE TIMES TO BLUFF

Just as there are times when it is correct to bluff, there are times when it is dead wrong to try it. There aren't that many different situations, but they occur often enough in hold'em that they are certainly worth mentioning. Here they are:

1. Any Flop That Has an Ace in It

Even though there may not be a preflop raise or a bet on the flop, it's just too likely that someone flopped a pair of aces and will call if you bet. In a ten-handed hold'em game, someone will be dealt an ace 86.7 percent of the time. That's about 7 out of 8 times. If an ace comes on the flop and you can't beat a pair of aces, especially if you're called, you're usually in trouble and are playing a guessing game. That's not the way to play poker.

2. Any Flop That Has a Jack or a 10

It is wrong to bluff any flop that has a jack *and* a 10 in it. Because of the fact that most players will play any two high cards, a jack and a 10 will either give them a pair or a draw to a good hand. And as we all know, any low-limit player who has a draw to a good hand cannot be bluffed out of the hand. Consider these two different flops: J♦ 10♥ 3♠ and 9♠ 5♦ 2♣. If you bet, which one of these flops will enable a player to call you?

3. With a Preflop Raise Only Semibluff

Do not attempt to bluff if there was a preflop raise unless you are semibluffing at the nuts or there are very few players in the hand. There are two good reasons for this:

   1. The preflop raiser could have anything and have you beat (you're drawing dead).

   2. The preflop raise created a "protected" pot.

Everyone knows that the raiser probably (statistically speaking) does not have a pair in the pocket and anyone who flopped a pair will call him down to the river. In that case, you don't have to beat just the raiser, you also have to beat the other caller.

4. Against Many Flop Callers

Don't attempt to bluff if there are many callers in to see the flop and you have only $2 in the hand. Learn to let it go and get on to the next hand.

Let's say you decide to bluff about 10 percent of the time. If every other player decides to bluff with the same frequency, then you might be facing a bluff from someone every other hand or so. How do you decide if the other player is bluffing when he bets? You can never know for sure, but there are a few indicators that might help you figure out where you stand. Here they are, in no particular order:

INDICATIONS THAT YOUR OPPONENT IS BLUFFING

1. When There Is No Straight or Flush Draw on the Flop

If there is a bettor all through the hand in this situation, he is probably not bluffing. He most likely has top pair with a good kicker on the flop, or an overpair. This is especially true if there was a preflop raise and another caller beside yourself. The bettor could have anything, but the caller has to have something.

In these cases, it's the caller you should be more fearful of than the bettor, especially if the bettor checked on the turn. It most likely means that he tried a bluff on the flop but since he got called in two spots, he decided to give up the bluff. The bettor could have anything since he could be bluffing, but the caller has to have something to call with.

2. When There Are Few Players in the Hand

The fewer the number of players that there are in the hand, especially on the river, the more likely the bettor is to be bluffing. The bettor won't always be bluffing just because there is only the two of you in the hand, but it is more likely than usual. This is particularly true if the river card did not fit in with the flop in any way. It means that anyone who had a draw on the flop missed and would have to bet to have a chance to win the hand.

3. If There Is Just You and One Other Player

Let's say there is just you and one other player on the river. Your opponent bets, and then as you start to call, he tells you that you can "save your money" or that he has the nuts. He's usually bluffing. If he really did have the nuts, why would he bet into you? All he would have to do is say, "Check," and then show you his cards. Usually, he will have bet because he could not check and win and when it started to look like he was going to be called, he had to do something to keep that from happening.

Like I said, if he really wanted you to "save your money," he'd check and show you his hand to save you that bet.

If you suspect that the player who just bet is bluffing, here are a few tips to help you decide what to do. He could be bluffing on the river if:

a. It only cost him one bet to try to steal the pot.

b. The pot is big.

c. He has to bluff only one player.

d. The river card did not help the possible draws that were represented on the flop.

e. The bettor raised before the flop and no aces or face cards came on the board.

f. Everyone checked on any round in the hand.

g. You just lost a big pot or two to the player who just now bet.

ADVERTISING BLUFFS

When you pull off a successful bluff, you should not show your hand if you don't have to, and you should not give any indications that you just won a pot by bluffing. If you're known to be a frequent bluffer, the other players will start checking their good hands to you and calling you on the river.

However, there are several reasons why you would want to advertise the fact that you just won a pot by bluffing. Here are a few reasons why you'd want to advertise your bluff:

1. You Want to Be Called When You Bet in the Future

This would be when you've decided that you're going to tighten up and bet only for value. You know that when you bet on the river in the future, you'll have a hand that can stand a call, but the other players won't be sure if you're bluffing or not. You'll know that you won't be.

2. Confusing a Player

You want to unnerve a player who's been beating up on you. Anything you can do to confuse him, and therefore interfere with his decision-making process, can only help you.

3. You've Played a Hand Out of Position

And you want everyone to know it. This is so that in the future, if you need to be holding some nonstandard cards in order to have a great hand, you want everyone to realize that you could have just that type of hand because they've already seen you play just such a hand out of position.

A player who bets before the dealer can turn the next card is not necessarily bluffing, but it usually indicates that he has a weak hand and is trying to convey strength. If he really did have a strong hand, it would be more reasonable to wait to see the next card before betting it right out. It only makes sense that he would want to assess the impact of the next card before deciding what to do. If his hand really was so good that he did not have to fear any card that could come, then he certainly would not want to give away that fact.

As obvious as it may sound, you will often be faced with having to call a bet from a player who is probably bluffing just because it is correct for him to attempt a bluff. In other words, there are situations that arise where you know a bettor is bluffing, he knows that you know that he's bluffing, and he bets anyway. It may be correct for him to bluff because of the cards on the board and the way the hand was played.

Most players will tell themselves in these situations, "Well, he's bluffing but I can't call anyway." You're right. What you should do is *raise*, especially if there's just the two of you. Believe me, it's very, very difficult for a player who's on a stone cold bluff to call when he's raised on the end. That's why you should try it once in a while.

CHAPTER SUMMARY

This has been a particularly long chapter, so I will summarize the main points for you:

Calling Before the Flop

Whether or not you should call before the flop depends on your position, the strength of your hand, the strength of the opposition, prior bets and raises, whether it's a loose or tight game, and whether you are winning or losing.

Raising Before the Flop

The number one thing that you can do to *immediately* improve your game is to quit routinely calling preflop raises unless you have a genuine raising hand.

The five major reasons to raise before the flop are:

1. To eliminate players.

2. To get value from your hand.

3. To gain information.

4. To bluff or semibluff.

5. To get a free (cheap) card.

Calling Preflop Raises

You need a strategy for calling preflop raises. This is what you should consider:

1. Who raised?

2. What position is the raiser in?

3. How many players have already called?

4. How many players are behind you?

5. Who might reraise behind you?

6. Are you on a draw?

7. Can you beat the raiser at this point?

Checking or Folding on the Flop

The flop is the time to get away from your hand if you're going to. You should usually check and fold if you flop nothing against several players. When you check and call, try to convey the impression that you have something but have decided to check anyway. Don't check out of turn because it induces bluffs against you.

Betting on the Flop

If you're equally undecided between checking or betting, you should usually bet. You should bet if you flop what you think is the best hand. Do not slowplay a set of aces. The more vulnerable that you think your hand is, the more inclined you should be to bet rather than check.

Raising on the Flop

A raise on the flop is not going to drive out a player who flopped any kind of draw at all. All you're going to do is build a pot. You should usually raise if you flop top pair with an ace kicker. Also you should usually raise from late position if you flop a good draw, because this often buys you one, and often two, free cards.

Playing on the Turn

You should have the probable best hand or a draw to the best hand to play on the turn. If you know that you're going to call on the turn and the river, you should occasionally raise on the turn with what would ordinarily be a calling hand.

Pot Odds and Calling on the River

To determine your pot odds, just divide the size of the bet you have to call into the size of the pot. If you can't decide between calling and folding on the river, you should call more as the pot gets bigger. Be aware that just calling on the end with the nuts can make you more money than raising, if you're in an early position. If you're going to check and call, you should consider betting it first.

Betting on the River

Bet your good hands right out for value rather than try to get fancy. Bet if the possible straight or flush draw did not get there on the river. Bet with nearly anything if it's been checked to you two or three times. Don't call an "Afraid You Won't Bet" bet without a great hand.

Split Pots

Don't play a hand from the beginning heads-up if it's very likely that you'll have a split pot. Always raise and reraise on the river with the nuts even if you do think you might have a split pot.

Check-Raising

Because check-raising makes players call two bets, it places an emphasis on building pots and driving players out of the hand. A player who check-raises to force you to call two bets cold usually wants you to fold, while a player who check-raises so as to let you call one bet and then another usually wants you to stay in the hand. You should check your good hands to aggressive players on your left. Players who flop fantastic hands usually wait for the turn to check-raise. A player who check-raises you on the turn definitely expects you to call.

Bluffing

Bluffing on the end is usually a simple matter of mathematics and pot odds. If you win most of the time that you try a bluff, you are not bluffing often enough. It is wrong to never bluff because you lose money by not betting when a bluff has a positive expectation. The bigger the pot is and the fewer the number of players you're facing, the more you should bluff. Do not bluff with an ace, jack or 10 on the flop. A player who bets with the certain knowledge that you'll call is usually not bluffing.

9

THE SCIENCE OF TELLS

If you always knew what your opponent's poker hand was after the last card is dealt, there would be one play that you would never make again on the river.

What do you think it is?

Obviously, you'd never have to just call again. You would always be able to either raise or fold, but never just call. Of course, you can't always know for sure what the other guy is holding, but you can usually have a pretty good idea judging from his position, his betting and calling and an educated guess using deductive reasoning. These clues are definitely better than nothing and sometimes you can put a player on exactly a certain hand.

But what if you can't? What if he's a good enough player to sufficiently disguise his possible holdings and therefore, make you play a guessing game? There is another method by which you can further reduce the number of his possible hands in your mind and it is through the use of tells.

A **tell** is a mannerism or a physical action that a poker player exhibits during the play of his hand which reveals that his hand is strong or weak. The tell can be either verbal or nonverbal and it can be either made on purpose or unconsciously. In poker, reading tells can be either very profitable or of not much value, depending upon the particular players and game conditions. In a limit game, most of your decisions will be based on simple mathematics and pot odds. Often, there will be times when you will be genuinely undecided about what to do at the end of the hand and will need more information than just the pot odds.

And there will be other times when you play a hand to the river with an opponent and will be certain of his hand. Then, at the last second, you'll see something that will make you say, "Whoa, wait a minute. He doesn't have what I thought he had because the tell I just caught is very reliable."

This is where being able to read a tell and knowing what it means is worth money to you. Here are a few beginning general guidelines for reading tells:

1. Weak When Strong, Strong When Weak

Most average low-limit players usually pretend to be strong when they are weak and pretend to be weak when they are strong. Think about it. How many times have you been in a game when the player who bet really acted disgusted with his hand, acted like he was ashamed to bet it and as soon as you called, showed you a full house? And how many times have you been in a hand with a player who bet and raised on every round from the beginning and, when you started to call on the end, announced he had a full house. But after you actually did call, said sheepishly, "I don't have anything. You win."

That's why I have emphasized throughout the book that you should usually act strong when strong and act weak when weak. Most players will all too readily assume that your display of obvious strength is an act, because that is the way they would play a weak hand. It doesn't occur to them that you are playing your hand strongly because you are strong. As the younger generation says, "Wow, what a concept." It works.

2. If You Spot a Tell

You should try to decide if it's an act or not. Is it a fake tell? Whatever it is, you should try to figure out what the other player wants you to do and then, if it's possible for you, do the opposite. It will be easier for you to decide on a player's intentions once you become more adept at reading tells.

3. Trust Your Instincts and Gut Reactions

Don't try to outsmart yourself or make the question to be answered more difficult. Your instincts are involuntary and instantaneous and therefore, unclouded by emotions or indecision. You will often be outplayed in this game, so there will be many times when your instincts are just wrong. But they are better than nothing if you have nothing else to go on.

4. Do They Like Their Hands?

Players may talk a lot about their hands, but they will rarely say exactly what their hand is. All you'll be able to tell is if they like their hands or not. It is tough to fake a genuine smile when you hold a probable loser, and it's difficult to hide your disappointment when you miss your draw to the nut flush on the river. You won't always know exactly what a player's exact hand is, but it sometimes won't be hard to tell if he likes his hand or not.

What follows is a list of the most common and useful tells in a low-limit game. Keep in mind that no tell is 100 percent reliable all of the time and you will often be seeing fake tells designed, of course, to fool you. Another thing that you will have to figure out is exactly what does a particular tell mean to a particular player? In other words, how reliable is the tell when you see it and does it mean something other than what it usually means?

Let me use a common tell as an example. It is a fact that in a low-limit game, players who talk and ramble on absentmindedly often clam up instantly when they get a great hand. When you see it happen, it usually means that the player did in fact just get a great hand.

But, perhaps there is a particular player who clams up every time he looks at his hole cards. Since he obviously can't be getting A♣ A♥ or K♠ K♥ every hand, this particular tell is not valid for this particular player. You'll have to perform this mental exercise for every combination of tells and players to know what's valid and what's not.

LIST OF TELLS
1. Players in Wheelchairs and Walkers
Players in wheelchairs and players who use walkers and canes intend to stay put once they get situated at the table and this in turn makes them more patient players than the average opponent. They may not be good poker players, but they will wait for what they consider to be the better hands. They don't often take chances by drawing for longshots. This is not a true tell in the purest sense of the word but it is something that you should know because it will help you put these players on a hand.

2. Neat and Conservative Players
Players who appear to be neat and conservative, both in dress and in their actions, also tend to play more conservatively. How they arrange their chips, their cash, and hold their cards are all reliable indicators of their frame of mind, and it spills over in how they play their hands.

3. Impatient Players
Impatience is usually a sign of a reasonably good hand. Anyone who asks, "Whose turn is it?" or says "Come on, let's play," or something like that, probably has a decent hand. If he intended to fold, he probably wouldn't care if it took a few extra seconds for the action to get to him.

4. Mannerism Changes

A player who has been slouching in his chair and then suddenly sits up when he sees his hole cards probably has a good hand. This is also true for players who wear reading glasses, but only when they intend to play their hands. A player who hurriedly puts out his cigarette, quickly finishes his drink, abruptly ends the conversation he's having, or summarily dismisses any spectators also probably has a good hand. You obviously don't need to do any of these things if you intend to fold your hand when it's your turn.

5. Players Showing Their Hands to Spectators

A player who lets a non-player see his hand at the beginning of play usually has a good hand, or at least one that he's not ashamed of. A player who shows his hand to a spectator at the end of the hand, and especially after he's bet on the river and is awaiting a call or fold from a single opponent, more likely has a bad hand. He will often show it in an effort to convince the potential caller that he has a good hand, and indeed, a hand that is so good that he's not afraid to show it. It's been my personal experience that a player who does this is often on a pure bluff and is afraid you'll call.

6. When A Good Player Makes His First Bet

When a good player does not play any of the first few hands dealt to him and then chooses to play his first hand, especially from an early position and he is not in the blind, he usually has a good hand, and more than likely, has at least one ace. Most good players like to win their first hand so they can then play with "your" money and not theirs.

7. Players Who Stare at the Flop

Players who continue to stare at the flop after it hits the table usually did not flop anything. They are looking at it in an attempt to find something that's not there, and that takes a little bit longer. Players that see the flop and then quickly and involuntarily glance at their chips and then quickly look back up at the flop, usually flopped a hand that they intend to bet. They're just checking to make sure their chips are still there.

Whenever I see this tell in a player, I'm reminded of the movie where the bad guys surprise the rich guy in his mansion and demand to know where the safe is. He will quickly and unknowingly glance at the appropriate picture hanging on the wall without saying anything. He didn't have to.

8. Players Who Cover Their Mouth

Players who casually and nonchalantly, yet unknowingly, cover their mouths after betting are usually bluffing. The act of betting and representing a good hand when in fact you have a garbage hand causes an unconscious internal conflict between your actions and what you know to be the truth. You may say, "Bet," but your subconscious knows differently and it will contradict your words.

9. Players Who Bet Forcefully or in an Exaggerated Style

A player who deliberately throws his chips into the pot in a forceful or obviously exaggerated manner is usually bluffing. He is trying to intimidate you with his many chips and his belligerent manner. A belligerent manner usually indicates strength but not at the poker table. If his hand was really that strong, he would be trying to gently coax you into calling instead of scaring you out of the hand.

10. Players Who Direct Their Bet Towards a Particular Player

Players who bet, but seem to throw their chips in the direction of a particular player instead of the customary position toward the pot, are usually weak and don't want to be called. This is called a *directed bet* and its purpose is to intimidate the player who the chips are thrown at. I have a personal policy of raising every other time that a directed bet is made at me and I often win the pot right there.

11. Players Who Intimidate Their Opponents

While we're on the subject of intimidating players, a player who stares at you when it is your turn to bet usually does not want you to bet. Staring is considered to be confrontational and the player who stares at you wants you to be meek and mild and not do anything that might be aggressive, like betting.

This tell is most often seen after the river card comes and there are just two players. The player who missed his draw will often noticeably raise his head from looking down at the flop, turn his head to the left or right and stare right at his sole opponent. In poker tell language, this means, "I missed my draw and don't you dare bet."

12. A Player Who Immediately Calls Your Bet

A player who calls your bet so fast that he almost has his chips in the pot before you do almost always has a weak calling hand. He is trying to impress you that he is so strong that he doesn't even have to think about calling. He's usually on a draw and wants his quick call to cause you to have second thoughts about betting on the next round.

13. A Player Who Reaches for His Chips Before You Bet

When a player behind you reaches for his chips to call before you've even acted on your hand, he usually does not intend to call. He wants you to think that he will readily call when in fact he does not want you to bet. He is trying to discourage your bet by making it apparent that you're going to be called anyway. If he really were going to call your bet, he wouldn't do anything to discourage you from betting. He is faking strength.

14. A Player Who Delays in Calling Your Bet

Often a player will call your bet, but only after taking a long time to make up his mind about it and letting you know that he really didn't want to call. If you determine that he's not acting, you should almost always bet it right out on the next round because there is a greater than average chance that he'll fold. He's usually looking for a miracle card to make a longshot draw and, as we all know, he'll miss most of the time.

15. Players Who Flash One of Their Hole Cards

Players who flash or expose one of their hole cards to you, generally have a weak hand and are trying to intimidate you. If his hand were really that good, he'd be very careful to conceal it and protect it. Why risk losing a call when everybody thinks you have the nuts—unless you really don't?

16. Tells on Fabulous-Looking Flops

Whenever there is a spectacular-looking uniform flop, you should pause a few seconds before acting and pay attention to the players who are *not* in the hand. We are talking about flops like Q♦ J♦ 10♦, K♣ K♦ K♠ or A♥ A♦ K♦. Often a player who threw away a key card that would go well with one of these flops will say or do something to give it away.

Many low-limit players who mucked a card that could have made a monster will moan, slap their forehead, roll their eyes in disgust, tell their neighbor, pound the table, or even actually announce what their hand was. This is also true for those times when the flop contains a pair.

It's really helpful when you hold K♠ K♣ and the flop

is Q♦ Q♥ 7♠ and one player not in the hand moans and says, "Damn." But you have to pause a second to give him time to do it. It's an almost 100 percent reliable tell because a player not in the hand has no reason to influence the play or outcome of a hand that he's not in.

17. A Player Who Unnecessarily Shows the Nuts at the End

A player who has the nuts and shows his hand at the end when he doesn't have to is often doing it because he intends to bluff in the very near future and wants you to know that he only shows down the nuts. He's trying to take advantage of his image as a winner before too many hands pass and his winning image fades in your memory.

18. A Player Who Coaxes Along an Opponent's End Decision

When a player bets on the end and then shows obvious, visible disappointment that his only opponent is not going to call, he usually does not have a good hand and actually does not want a call. When the potential caller moves from being undecided to leaning towards not calling, the bettor gets in gear and "helps" him by assuring him that he's about to make the right decision. If the bettor's hand was really that good, he'd be doing everything he could to get a call from his sole opponent.

19. A Player Showing Visible Disappointment

One of the most common tells on the end is when a player was on a straight or flush draw to the nuts, and missed. He will often have a big letdown in that he will exhale deeply, slouch down in his chair and have a genuinely sad look on his face. He may actually tell you he missed his hand. He might even turn his cards face up as a gesture of folding, throw his cards down on the table in disgust, curse, hit the table or even throw his cards in the muck with great enthusiasm.

The secret is that you have to pause a second on the end to give him a chance to do one of these things. If you immediately check upon seeing the river card, you may have cost yourself an opportunity to bluff when you had an almost 100 percent chance of success.

10

SKILLS YOU NEED TO WIN AT TEXAS HOLD'EM

Obviously, it takes more than being able to sit at a table for long periods of time and throw chips into the pot to be a good poker player. You need certain specific skills to be good at this game. Most of the skills you need have already been mentioned directly or indirectly in the examination of another topic.

This section is devoted exclusively to examining the specific skills that you need to be a good hold'em player. There are no big secrets in this list. My purpose is to get you to think about poker as a game that does require certain skills, and to make you realize that you can improve on those skills if you concentrate on them individually.

Here's my list of skills that you need to be a good poker player:

1. Game Selection
If you are the 10th best poker player in the world, then you are better than 99.999999 percent of all the other poker players (assuming one billion players). But, if you choose to take the one empty seat in a ten-handed game where the other players are the first through ninth best players in the world, then you would be the worst player in the game.

You might as well be rated near the bottom of the world's worst players if you can't beat anyone in your game. In this example, you went from being 10th in the entire world to worst in your game, and what caused it? Game selection.

Being good at game selection means choosing a game you can expect to beat.

2. Seat Selection

Because money tends to move clockwise in most poker games, and especially in hold'em, it is important that players with certain characteristics act on their hands before you. You want both very loose and very tight players to sit on your immediate right as well as players with a lot of money on the table for the stakes that you're playing. You want all betting and raising to be completed before the action gets to you.

3. Mental Preparation

This includes a desire to succeed, patience, concentration, good judgment, and self-discipline. Your goal is to win. Don't give in to the temptation to play hands just for the sake of playing. Stay focused on the task at hand. Make your decisions based on the relevant facts available to you at the time. Have the desire to put it all together to work toward making good decisions.

4. Stay Educated

Stay abreast of developments in game theory and research. Share information with other poker players and read poker related literature.

5. Hand Selection

Your first decision, on whether you should enter the pot with your starting cards, is the most critical. This is actually what makes you a loser or winner in hold'em.

6. Buying a Free Card

Actually, you are raising on a cheap round in order to get a free card later during the more expensive round. This saves you one-half of one big bet and adds up over thousands of hands played.

7. Semibluffing and Bluffing

There are times when it's correct to bet with a hand you know is not the best. If you were to play only when you actually had the best hand you would get no action when you did play.

8. Raising and Check-Raising

You must know when to get the worse hands out and when to make them pay to beat you. If a player beats you with a hand that he would not have called a raise with, you've made a serious mistake.

9. Reading Hands and Reading Tells

Both of these skills used in unison will give you the best chance of estimating what your opponents are holding, and once you know that, you will always be able to play your hands perfectly.

10. Your Skill at Deception

Deception is not a major part of low-limit hold'em because so many players don't have the poker smarts to know that you are using deception in the play of your hand. But, there are times when you can win a big pot if you have varied your play in a critical situation.

11. Slowplaying

Slowplaying works well because you are playing your hand in a weak manner on an early round in order to disguise your hand and make more money on a later round.

12. Adjusting to Game Conditions

Poor players may leave the game and be replaced by rocks. Players with all the money may leave the game. The game may get short-handed. It may be later than you think. Any number of things could change so that it may not be the same original good game that you started out playing six hours ago. Be alert for changing game conditions.

13. Knowing When to Quit

There is no reason you should have to stay and play after you've won or lost a certain amount of money. You should play as long as you have a positive expectation in the game and leave when you don't, whatever the reason may be. This is especially true in a casino game.

One final word about the skills you need to play this game: More money is lost by players who know what the right thing to do is, but don't do it, than for any other reason. Having a strategy, a game plan and the discipline to stick to it are, along with a sufficient bankroll, the four most important things that a player needs to be a winner at Texas hold'em. You cannot be a winner if you're missing any one of these four essential ingredients.

11

HOW TO PLAY SPECIFIC HANDS

In most poker books, the part about how to play each hand is usually at the front of the book. I deliberately chose to put this part at the end because I thought it important to first explain all of the elements that go into the playing of a hand.

When I advise you how to play a certain hand in a certain position, you will already have a good understanding of the concepts of position, raising, check-raising, slowplaying, bluffing, semibluffing, reading hands, tells, and adjusting to game conditions. This final chapter is meant to help you bring it all together in your mind so that you can see how all of these abstract concepts work in actual practice.

I am going to give you some specific advice about how to play specific hands and I'll try to tell you everything that you'll need to know about the hand. I don't want you to say a few years from now, "Boy, I wish he'd told me that could happen when I had A♦A♣ in the pocket," or whatever the hand is. As I said in the introduction, I'll try to tell you everything that I wish someone had told me when I first started playing this game.

I am not going to discuss all 169 different possible hands. I believe that if you've read the book this far, you will already know how to play hands like K♦ 5♠, J♠ 3♣, 7♣ 2♦ and hands like this. There is almost no difference in how you would play a flopped set of eights or sevens, and the same general principles hold when you flop the nuts, whether you're holding A♦ Q♥ or 10♠ 9♣. There is also almost no difference in how you would play a hand like A♦ 7♦ or A♥ 6♥.

We will concentrate on those hands that have a positive expectation and you would at least see the flop with most of the time. Here goes:

1. A♦ A♥

A pair of aces in the pocket is the best hand you can have in hold'em. There is no other hand that will win more money, hand in and hand out in the long run. You should usually raise preflop every time you get them from any and all positions and you should definitely reraise if possible. If you're not willing to put in the maximum number of bets with the best hand in Texas hold'em, then you should ask yourself why you're even playing the game. Anyone who calls you is definitely taking long odds to beat you. Here is a list of things to keep in mind regarding aces in the pocket:

> **a.** You are about a 4 to 1 favorite over any other player holding a pocket pair if you both play to the river. You will flop another ace 10.5 percent of the time and you will flop a full house about 1 percent of the time.

> **b.** You are a 2 to 1 favorite against a single opponent on a straight or a flush draw. You are a slight favorite over two players who are trying to make straights or flushes against you. If you hold A♣ A♠ and flop two more clubs or spades, you will make a backdoor flush only 3.33 percent of the time.

> **c.** Most low-limit players who have A♥ A♣ in the pocket will raise before the flop and then

carefully watch each player call the raise in turn. He will often actually bounce his head up and down in a clockwise motion as the action goes around the table. He's doing this to make sure that each player puts the correct amount of money into what he thinks of as "his" pot. This is a reliable tell in low limit.

d. Most players will call all bets and raises on the flop when they hold A♠ A♦ in the pocket, even when they know that they're beat. This is especially true if the player is on a rush, is winning, or is drinking.

e. If you hold A♦ A♠ and get a safe-looking flop with several players, you do not want the top card on the flop to pair up on the turn or river. It's just too likely to have made the caller trips to beat you. The higher the paired card, the more likely it is to hurt you. For example, a flop of Q♦ 10♠ 3♥ with the Q♣ on the turn will be more likely to beat you than a flop of 8♠ 5♥ 3♣ with an 8♣ on the turn.

f. You should be alert for the possibility that an ace on the turn or river is an out for another player. For example, you hold A♠ A♣ and the flop is K♥ J♦ 5♠. An ace on the turn could possibly make a straight for someone holding Q♦ 10♠. In low-limit games, this is also possible for a flop like 10♣ 3♦ 2♠ because most low-limit players will see the flop with any 5♣ 4♣.

g. You hold A♦ A♥ and the flop is A♣ 2♠ 2♥. You will usually win the hand, but anyone holding a deuce has a 4.3 percent chance of making four of kind by the river. It does happen and it's okay if you're in a jackpot game. I would not slowplay this hand because of the potential for getting second-best hands to call you down and pay you off. Anyone holding the other ace or a deuce will certainly not fold.

h. You hold A♠ A♣ and the flop is A♥ Q♦ 10♠. Do not slowplay because of the obvious straight draw. Anyone who has a one card draw to the straight will pay you off. Do not let him draw for free.

i. You hold A♦ A♣ and the flop is A♥ 9♥ 3♣. Even though there is a possible straight draw to the bicycle, it is not likely. You can slowplay or check-raise with this hand because the turn card is not likely to hurt you.

j. You hold A♦ A♥ and the flop is three more diamonds or hearts. You have an overpair, the probable best hand at this point, and a nut four flush. I almost always bet it right out in this situation because many players holding a single diamond or heart will call hoping to make his flush. Anyone holding top pair with a good kicker will likely pay you off as well as anyone on a straight draw. You will often get called when you bet on the flop just because other players will think that you are weak and would check if you flopped a great hand like this. Make them pay for this bad judgment. If you check, they cannot make a mistake by checking after you. However, if you bet, they can make a mistake by calling you.

k. If you have a pair of aces in the pocket and get a good-looking flop, you would like one of two things to happen:

> **1.** You get another ace and maybe make a full house, or

> **2.** Run off a small pair on the turn and end.

l. If you know for a fact that another player has a pair of aces in the pocket, you have the best chance of beating him if you hold any one of these hands: J♦ J♥, the other two aces, 10♠ 10♣, Q♦ J♦, J♥ 10♥, 7♦ 6♦ and 6♣ 5♣. You are still not a favorite over pocket aces, but experience and computer analysis suggest that these are the hands that can beat aces.

m. If you know for a fact that another player has a pair of aces in the pocket, you will lose the most money if you play with any of the following hands: An ace with any suited card, A♦ K♥, A♣ Q♠, an ace with any other card, a king and any other card, and all small pairs.

2. A♣ K♣, A♣ Q♣, A♣ J♣, A♣ 10♣

Two cards to the nut royal flush draw. When you hold one of these hands this is what you'll get on the flop:

A. An ace or your other card	28.960%
B. An ace and your other card	2.021%
C. Flopped flush	.837%
D. Flopped royal flush	.005%
E. Two more aces or kings	1.300%
F. Two more of your suit	10.944%
G. Four to a straight	7.930%
H. Full house	.092%
Total	52.089%

When you hold two big suited cards you will flop something to go with them 52 percent of the time. If you have raised before the flop, or if you have position, or if you're heads-up, you have an even greater advantage. However, in low-limit hold'em, you will often have to make a hand to win the pot. It is only as you play progressively higher limits that you will be able to win more often just by betting and using your position.

The play of these hands is pretty straightforward. You either flop a playable hand, a draw, or nothing. Your draws will usually be to the nuts. If you flop nothing, your decision to play beyond the flop is determined by your position, the size of the pot, and your estimate of the chances of bluffing successfully. The only thing you have to fear is that the board will pair.

If you are in early position, I recommend that you usually just call before the flop for several good reasons. You have a hand that can make the nuts several ways and I don't think you should drive out your customers when they could make second-best hands that will pay you off. Also, if you don't raise, you can see the flop as cheaply as possible and then get out if you miss, which will happen 48 percent of the time.

If you hold A♣ Q♣ and flop a queen, there will also be

a king on the flop 2.5 percent of the time. It is 6.5 to 1 that you had the best hand before the flop. If you hold A♦ J♦, it is only 3.5 to 1 that you have the best hand before the flop. Keep in mind that any ace-high straight draw will always be a gutshot straight draw.

3. A♥ 9♥ Down Through A♥ 2♥

These suited hands just do not perform as well as you might think. The fact that it is a suited hand only helps you an additional 3 percent of the time and some of those times you'll still lose with your flush.

Ironically, computer analysis shows that A♠ 5♠ and A♠ 4♠ win more often and make more money than A♥ 8♥ and A♥ 7♥. That is because you can make a straight with the wheel cards much more easily than you can with the other cards. You should not routinely call preflop raises with these hands, especially if you have poor position or there are very few players in the hand. You need a lot of players in the hand to get the right odds to play these drawing cards.

If you hold an ace and a small suited card such as a deuce, this is what you'll get on the flop:

A. Aces up	2.02%
B. Trip aces or your other card	1.35%
C. Flush	.84%
D. Straight	.32%
E. Full house	.09%
F. Four aces or deuces	.01%
Total	4.63%

This shows that you'll totally miss the flop over 95 percent of the time—assuming that a pair of aces or deuces will not help you. And you still face the unpleasant possibility that you can make aces-up and still lose the hand.

4. A♥ K♠

It's 20 to 1 that no one else holds A♦ A♣ or K♠ K♥ in the pocket. One advantage that it has over A♣ K♣ is that you can make one of two flushes when four more of your suit hits the board, which happens only about 5 percent of the time. Another advantage of not being suited is that it's more difficult to flop a four flush (2.245 percent versus 10.944 percent when suited), which in turn, makes it easier to fold if you have to.

If you flop an ace or king, you should definitely bet, and if there's a bet before you, you should raise to help protect your hand. You will have top pair with top kicker and you'll usually have the best hand at this point. Be wary if the board pairs and a player who was previously a caller now bets.

5. All Other Hands With an Ace

How you play these hands containing an ace is crucial to your success as a hold'em player because they constitute about 15 percent of the hands you'll be dealt. Most players almost always see the flop whenever they hold an ace and this makes them big losers in the long run.

You should normally enter the pot only with A♦ K♣, A♥ Q♠, A♣ J♠ and A♥ 10♦. You should not play with A♦ 9♣ and below because they just don't win often enough to show a profit in the long run. For example, if you are dealt an ace in a ten-handed game, there's a 75 percent chance that another player also has been dealt an ace. You're a big underdog if his kicker is higher than yours. If you have something like A♥ 6♠ and get an ace on the flop, and get action, then you're probably beat and are playing a guessing game. That's not the way to play winning poker.

Since most players do play every hand with an ace, be careful when the flop has two or three wheel cards in it. If you have A♦ K♠ and the flop is K♥ 3♦ 5♠ and you get a lot of callers, you have a problem hand. It looks like any little card could make someone a wheel and that's probably what will happen. This is especially true if there were no preflop raises. This makes it more likely that someone is holding an ace and a wheel card.

If you have ace-little in one of the blinds and it's raised before the flop, you should throw it away even though you already have a small investment in the pot. You probably do not have the best hand at this point since the raiser doesn't figure to have a worse hand than yours. Don't get tied to the hand just because you already have $1 invested. This is especially true if there are many other players who have already called the raiser in front of you.

If there are one or more preflop raises, and you hold A♦ Q♥, you could very well lose a lot of money if you flop an ace and play all the way to the river. There is a good chance that the raiser has A♣ A♦, K♥ K♠, Q♦ Q♥ or A♠ K♦. And if he doesn't, one of the other callers probably does.

If an ace or king flops, you are practically drawing dead. If you get a queen on the flop, you will have a pair of queens with an ace kicker, but for you to have the best hand, the raiser would have to have raised before the flop with something like A♥ J♠, A♥ 10♦, K♠ Q♦, K♣ J♥, Q♣ J♥ or Q♦ 10♠. That's not too likely.

A♦ Q♥ is a classic trap hand when there's a preflop raise, and you should learn to be careful with it. You have to know your players and what they are likely to raise with and not raise with before the flop.

One good thing about playing two of the top five cards is that any straight draw to the ace-high straight will be the nuts. You will rarely have to split the pot because you'll be using both of your hole cards. Keep in mind that the higher the cards are on the board, the more likely it is that someone can and will make the nut straight. This is due to the fact that players are more likely to play the higher cards necessary to make this straight.

On the other hand, the lower the highest card on the board, the more likely it is that someone has made a small straight. For example, if the board is 2♦ 4♥ 5♠ 7♣ 9♥ and there is a lot of action, you can be certain that someone made the straight. But, when the board is something like K♥ 5♥ 8♠ J♣ 4♠ and there is a lot of action, it's less likely that someone made a straight even though it's possible.

If you flop an ace-high straight, you should almost always bet it for value because this is exactly the type of flop that will make other second-best hands pay you off. Someone will usually have what they think is the nuts (even though a straight is possible) and someone else will probably be on a draw to a better hand than your straight. Make them pay to beat you. Anyone holding a straight draw, top pair with top kicker, two pair, trips or a flush draw will usually be there until the river. Don't let 'em play for free.

If you have A♦ K♠, A♥ Q♠, A♣ J♦ or A♠ 10♦ and you flop two pair, you definitely have to bet. If your opponent has a hand, you want him to pay to draw to a better hand. If he is on a draw you also want him to pay. If you hold A♥ J♣ and flop A♦ J♥ 6♠, the next card could make someone else a straight. The turn card could also give someone a draw at an open-end straight or a four flush to draw to.

Remember, the flop is when many players decide to muck their hand if they don't flop anything and there's a bet. Don't let them see the turn card and pick up a draw for free if you can help it. Giving a free card after the flop when you have any kind of hand at all is one of the classic beginner mistakes you'll see in this game, especially in a low-limit game where it seems everybody plays every hand.

If the flop has a big card in it, such as Q♥ 8♣ 6, and there is an ace on the turn or river, it often means that someone has made aces and queens. This also holds true when the ace is on the flop and the face card comes on the turn or river. If this happens and everyone checks on the turn, especially if there are many players, it usually means that someone was going to check-raise, but there was no bet to raise.

When this happens and there is a bet on the end, the

position of the bettor is very important. The worse (earlier) his position is, the more likely it is that he has a legitimate, powerful hand.

Think about it: He called before the flop from an early position. That means he more likely than not has two big cards in the hole. He bet or called on the flop when there was an ace or face card on board. He checked on the turn because, if he does have the good hand, his early position makes it more likely that a check-raise attempt will be successful.

A player in early position check-raises more often than a player in late position. He bet on the river into a large field from an early position with a large pot. He knows he's going to be called. All of this adds up to he fact that he has a very good hand.

If you have A♥ 7♣ and the flop is 8♠ 7♦ 2♥, you are much more likely to have the best hand than if the flop were K♥ J♣ 7♠ simply because players are more likely to throw away an 8 before the flop than they are a king or jack. You will often have the best hand and should usually bet it for value, especially if it's checked to you on the flop. With two cards to come, you have a 20.4 percent chance of improving to aces up or trips, and you might win without improving.

This is a common situation in hold'em and you should learn to take advantage of it. If you get called, you are probably looking at a straight draw or a pair of eights with a bad kicker.

Again, you have to know your players. If a good player calls your bet, you should probably abandon the lead. Check and fold if this good player bets it. If you're in a very loose game where everybody plays everything, you might consider pushing it if you think your opponents are on a draw.

In a single eight-hour session you will be dealt at least one ace about forty-eight times. Unfortunately, most of these hands will be trap hands if you play them. A hand with an ace in it gives you more opportunities to save money and not make mistakes that you know the other players will make. Namely, they'll play every hand with an ace and you won't. This is one easy way that you can save a lot of money in the long run and plug a big leak in your game.

It's so important that I think it needs to be said again: How you play hands with an ace is so important and such a big part of your game that you should learn to do it right, and that usually means *not* playing the hand. If you are dealt the A♦, then there are fifty-one other cards that can go with it and only about twenty of them are playable most of the time. Think about it.

6. K♠ K♥ and Q♦ Q♣

With these pairs, you will usually have the best hand before the flop, regardless of your position, but your position does have an influence on how you play the hand.

Let's look at having K♥ K♦ on the button. If several callers limp in then it is likely that at least one of them has an ace in the pocket. Whether you limp in to see the flop cheaply or raise to get more money in the pot in a hand you expect to win is a trade-off between saving money and building big pots.

Since an ace will come on the flop about 22 percent of the time, you may want to save your money and see the flop before you invest too much in the hand. This will give you an opportunity to get away from the hand for only one bet if you want to. You especially might want to play it like this if you're losing during this session or you've taken a few bad beats recently.

As your position improves and there are fewer, or perhaps no players in the hand, you should usually raise to narrow the field and increase your chances of winning the hand. You'll win smaller pots on average, but you will win more often. Better to have a 75 percent chance of winning a $50 pot than just a 15 percent chance of winning a $100 pot. When you raise with more players already in the pot, you will have bigger swings in your bankroll because of the decreased chance of eventually winning.

You will be a big winner in the long run with K♣ K♦ regardless of position, number of opponents, or number of raises. There is probably no wrong way to play this hand before the flop, but there is a way to play that will save you some money in the long run. Slow down with this hand in late position and be willing to throw it away if you feel you have to. Again, try not to make the mistake of calling with it after the flop (when you're sure you're beat) just because it is pocket kings.

If you have pocket K♥ K♣ in big or small blind position, I recommend that you do not exercise your raise option before the flop. You're not going to drive anyone out by making them call just one more bet. Your raise will give away the fact that you have a great hand and, of course, you'll be at a positional disadvantage throughout the hand.

There is one situation that occurs only 1.4 percent of the time, but is worth mentioning because of the concept involved. That is when you have K♠ K♣ and the flop has two or even three aces in it. I want to tell you that, from both a statistical viewpoint and my own personal experience, when you have pocket kings, one ace on the flop is usually bad for you, but two aces on the flop is usually good for you. I know it's counterintuitive, however, one more ace on the board means that there is one less ace available to be in someone's hand. Bet it right out and expect to win more often than if the flop had only one ace.

The difference between having K♥ K♦ and Q♣ Q♠ is not that great, but there are a few subtle points to be aware of. With queens, you'll get one or more overcards on the flop about 41 percent of the time. With no overcard on the flop, an overcard will be dealt on the turn or river 32 percent of the time. This means that your hand is more vulnerable and you'll be less likely to like the flop. For this reason, you should usually see the flop as cheaply as possible and be prepared to muck the hand in the face of a bad flop or a very large field.

If there is a preflop raise, you should usually just call. You don't gain that much by reraising. The raiser has two ways to beat you: He can already have you beat before the flop, or he can get help on the flop. Usually, you'd like to see the flop as cheaply as possible with Q♦ Q♥. Even if the raiser has A♥ K♣, you are only a slight 52 percent to 48 percent favorite. In any event, if you throw away your kings most of the time you see an ace on the flop, you are definitely saving the chips in your stacks and not losing that much in the long run.

One final word about pocket kings and queens. They are the only pairs with which you can flop a set and still end up with the nuts without improving. In other words, it is possible to flop a set of kings or queens and not be facing a possible straight or flush. An example of this would be a board of K♦ J♥ 8♠ 5♣ 2♥.

Most beginning low-limit players usually do not know how to play when they flop a set. They're so excited over having flopped a great hand that they don't think about how to maximize a possible win or minimize a possible loss. However, the most important thing to consider when you flop a set is the threat posed by the other two odd cards. For example, if you have K♦ K♥ and the flop is K♣ 7♥ 2♦, you are not looking at any possible straight or flush draws. A check is probably called for because a free card is not likely to hurt you and you need to give the other players more of a hand with which to call. A check from you might also induce another player to try to bluff at the pot.

On the other hand, if you have K♥ K♦ and the flop is K♣ J♣ 8♠, you should definitely bet to make the straight and flush draws pay to beat you. You're not going to lose anyone who flopped top pair or a straight or flush draw, but you can make them pay to draw and perhaps give them the wrong odds to play their hands.

The same guideline applies when you flop trips that is not a set. For example, you have A♠ 10♠ and the flop has two more tens. Whether or not you should bet depends on that one odd card that came with the two tens. If it's a big card or a card that makes a possible straight or flush draw, you should bet. With a flop like K♥ 10♥ 10♦, you will be called by anyone holding a king, two hearts or two cards to a straight draw. You are also a big favorite over anyone holding the other 10. Do not let them play for free. Getting players with second-best hands to put money in the pot is the essence of all forms of poker.

If you have the same A♠ 10♠ and the flop is 10♥ 10♦ 2♣, you have a much different situation. Now, instead of the other players having second-best hands, they very likely have no hand at all. You should usually check and give them a free card that will hopefully make them a second-best hand.

Anyone who picked up a draw on the turn will still be a huge underdog to you with only one more card to come.

An exception to slowplaying this hand on the flop is when there was a raise before the flop. That raise means it is more likely that someone already has a second-best hand on the flop and they will call if you bet. Most players who hold a pocket pair higher than tens will usually call you all the way to the river. Even so, don't forget that they would have an 8.4 percent chance of hitting their pair to make a big full house against you.

Also, if you have a 10 and get two more tens on the flop, you should be more inclined to bet as your kicker gets worse. In other words, check when you have A♣ 10♣ but bet when you have 10♥ 3♠. Again, if they're going to draw out on you, don't let 'em do it for free.

7. J♦ J♣ Down Through 2♦ 2♠

Pairs of jacks down through deuces are hands that usually need improvement to win, especially against many opponents. In other words, you should flop a set, an open-end straight draw (without drawing to the low end) or have no overcards on the flop to continue with the hand. If you do flop a set, you cannot make the nuts without improving after that. But that doesn't mean that you should fear every possible threat, especially if the turn and river had to hit perfect-perfect to present the threat.

For example, you hold 9♥ 9♦ and the flop is 9♠ 5♣ 2♦ and the turn and river are two more spades, clubs or diamonds. Don't slowplay if there's a possible straight or flush draw on board.

This is true for all threats on the board. It's not a legitimate threat unless it's likely that your opponent holds the cards needed to go with the board. In other words, there's just you and a single player who raised before the flop and you hold K♥ K♣. The flop is 7♣ 6♣ 3♣. You probably still have the best hand. Even though the board looks threatening, you're facing only one player and his preflop raise indicates he probably doesn't hold the cards needed to make the threat a real concern for you. Actually, the only card you need to worry about is the A♣ and if he does have it, it is still 2-1 against him making the flush.

You should usually not even call with pairs smaller than 9♣ 9♥. You need a near perfect flop to continue playing and win the hand. You don't lose that much in possible winnings by not playing these pairs, but you sure can lose a lot with them. If you must play small pairs, play them only in late position with a lot of callers in front of you and don't call a double bet cold with them.

8. Any Two Suited Cards

If you have two suited cards, you will flop a flush draw only one out of nine times. This means that the strength of your hand will come from their ranks. If you miss your flush, K♦ J♦ will still win the hand more often than 7♦ 4♦. You cannot play these purely drawing hands in an early position and you cannot play them with very few players in the pot because of the poor pot odds. This is not a good hand to call a preflop raise with because the raise means that you're most likely already beat and will be fighting an uphill battle.

The best advice I can give you about this type of hand is this: If you wouldn't play it if it were not suited, then you should play it only under the best of circumstances when it is suited. That means you need good position, a lot of players to see the flop, and the likelihood of winning a huge pot if you do hit your hand.

9. Two Cards to a Straight

If you start with two cards to a straight, the odds are you won't end up with the straight. The higher the cards are, the better your chances are of winning. It will take some experience and judgment to know if your top pair is any good and if your kicker is any good. If you flop top two split pair (no pair on the board), you will usually be the favorite to win the hand. Any open-end straight draw will usually be playable until the river unless the board pairs and there's a lot of action. A three or four flush on the board usually means trouble if you're drawing to a straight.

Most of the hands in this category are usually clear-cut calls, checks, bets and folds for you. As an easy rule of thumb, the final size of the pot has to be at least $80 in a $4/$8 game to justify drawing to an inside straight after the flop. And that's if, in your judgment, the hand will stand up if you do hit it.

HOW TO PLAY WITH A PAIR ON THE FLOP

There will be a pair on the flop about 12 percent of the time. How you play this hand is very important because, even though it doesn't happen often, you can lose a lot of money if you're not careful. Here's a list of things to keep in mind when the flop is paired:

1. The Strength of the Pair

The higher the pair on the flop, the more likely it is that someone has made trips. Players just play high cards more often than low cards.

2. The Number of Players in to See the Flop

The more players there are to see the flop, the more likely it is that someone flopped trips. Assume that the flop is J♦ 3♥ 3♠. A player who was dealt 9♣ 3♦ would have folded before the flop. But, if there are a lot of players to see the flop, then it's more likely that someone has a 3♣ or 3♦ with another card that would induce him to play the hand. The most obvious holding would be A♣ 3♣. The more players dealt into the hand, the more likely it is that someone will get a hand with which to play a 3.

3. Players Who Might Have Trips

Most players who flop trips in this situation will check, hoping to disguise their hand and hoping that someone else will bet it for them. They will then attempt a check-raise on the turn.

4. A Player Who Doesn't Have Trips

The player who usually doesn't have trips is usually the one who actually starts the betting. It's usually the player who just calls who really does have the trips. Seems backwards, but that's the way it is in $1-$4, $1-$5, $3/$6, $1-$4-$8-$8 games. This is less true as you play higher limits.

5. Don't Be Lulled into a False Sense of Security

Don't be lulled into a false sense of security when there's no bet on the flop or turn and you pick up a straight or flush draw. You could already be beat and if you're not, you could be beat on the river.

6. If There are Just a Few of You in the Hand

If there are just a few of you in the hand, you shouldn't play, because you're getting terrible pot odds. Wait for a better hand to put your money in. Since you really can't be sure what a check or a bet on the flop really means, why make a guessing game out of it? Wait for a hand where you want to put your money in the pot, not when someone else wants you to do that.

7. The Value of the Paired Card Is Very Important

Which one of these two flops do you think represents more of a threat to you: 9♥ 5♠ 5♦ or 6♠ 5♥ 5♦? Is a player more likely to play a 9♣ 5♥ or 6♣ 5♦? Whenever you see a pair on the board, you should think of the cards immediately above and below it and an ace. If a player does have a 5, in this example, his kicker is most likely an ace, 6 or a 4. That's because if he does have the 5, his most likely hand is A♣ 5♠, 6♠ 5♦ or 4♣ 5♠. He's not likely to play K♦ 5♠ or something like that.

You should be on the lookout for one of his likely hole cards to hit on the turn or river.

8. Only Two Other Players at Most Can Have Flopped Trips

If there are more than two players in the hand, you have to try to figure out what they likely have, based on their position, playing habits, bets and raises. If there are four or more players betting and calling on the flop or turn, you need a great hand to continue playing. Drawing to a straight or flush under these circumstances will cost a lot of money in the long run. You're drawing dead.

9. If You Do Make the Straight or Flush on the Turn

Do *not* slowplay a straight or flush if you make them on the turn. For you to be beat, someone had to have flopped trips and then made the full house on the turn. Use your judgment and carefully evaluate the board in determining if you're beat or not. That turn card is important as explained in the previous paragraph.

10. If You Intend to Bluff at the Pot

If, in your judgment, no one has one of the paired cards on the board, wait for the turn if you think a free card won't hurt you. Your opponent might be getting the right odds to call $4 on the flop if the pot is only $60 or $80, but he won't be getting the right odds to call $8 on the turn if there's only $60 or $80 in the pot.

11. If It's Checked on the Flop and on the Turn

If it's checked on the flop and the turn and there are a lot of players who get to see the river card for free, anything is possible. Don't be surprised to see a full house and a flush in the same hand. Players will be making hands that they wouldn't ordinarily make if they had to pay to play.

12. Reread Tell #16 in "The Science of Tells" Chapter

It pays to be alert.

13. If the Board Has Two Pair After the Turn

You almost can't pay to play if you're drawing to a straight or a flush. Don't be fooled if it's checked to you on the turn. If the other player has made his full house, you have nothing to gain and everything to lose if you bet. If you have the best hand, you win nothing because he can't call. And obviously, if you're beat, you lose. You should also check on the river for just this reason. Don't forget that you could be being set up for a check-raise on the river.

A player who checks and calls when the board has two pair is not necessarily checking because he has nothing. It might be because he only has the small end of the full house and doesn't want to get raised if he bets.

HOW TO PLAY WHEN YOU FLOP A FLUSH

The higher your flush, the less vulnerable your hand. Unless you have some specific reason to believe that a check-raise attempt will work or that you should slowplay the hand, you should usually bet it right out. Flushes are one of those hands that produce a higher than usual number of second-best hands and drawing hands.

If you flop a flush and bet, you will be called more often than usual, but on the other hand you will be drawn out on a little more often than usual. That's because the players on a flush draw won't believe that you flopped the flush and the only other types of hands that can call will be pairs, two pair and trips.

If a fourth or even a fifth card of your suit shows up, be alert for the straight flush. Making a straight flush in any one given hand is very unlikely but if you stipulate that you can start with five cards of the same suit and up to ten players can add two more cards to those five, then it becomes easy to make a straight flush. This is especially true when the lowest card on the board is relatively high, such as a 5 or 6. This is also true when three or four of the cards are close in rank.

The play of a flopped flush is pretty much straightforward: Make them pay to beat you. The lower your flush, the more vulnerable your hand. Any card of your suit can kill your hand unless you have an open-end straight flush draw to go with your flush. Because of that fact, you must bet. If a flush card comes on the river and you know that someone has made the flush, but you can't figure out who it was, I want to tell you that more often than not, it's the player who checked and called throughout the hand and is now betting into you.

The player who flopped a hand will bet to protect his cards. The player on the draw will usually check and call. If the caller raises on the end, you can be sure he made his hand.

HOW TO PLAY WHEN YOU FLOP TWO PAIR

If you have A♥ J♠ and the flop is A♦ J♥ 5♣, then your hand plays itself. Bet or check-raise if the guy on your left bets out of turn. Any straight draw and any ace will pay you off. For that matter, any time you flop top two pair, you will usually have the best hand and you should bet it.

If you flop top two pair and there are many players, and a lot—and I mean a lot—of raising, you are probably beat. Here is what has likely happened: If you flopped top two pair as in the above example, someone else flopped a set of fives. Considering the cards that are out, it's easier to flop a set of fives than it is to flop a set of aces or jacks. In any case, you are beat. For you to still have the best hand, the raiser would have to have a hand worse than yours and that means something like A♣ 5♠ or J♥ 5♦. He certainly wouldn't bet like that with just one pair.

If you have A♥ 7♥, the flop is A♣ 7♦ 3♠, and another player has A♠ K♣, you are a 14-1 favorite over him.

If you flop bottom two pair, you should definitely bet, because this hand doesn't figure to hold up very well against several players. Ideally, you want to win this hand on the flop because almost any card on the turn could beat you.

Any card higher than your two pair represents an obvious threat to your hand. The only improvement you can make is to a full house, and under the circumstances, you might be drawing dead.

Play carefully if you make a full house like this. That's just the nature of the game; two low pair makes a low full house and two high pair makes a higher full house. This concept comes into play when the flop has three cards to an ace-high straight and two players flop two pair, but a different two pair.

Here are a few miscellaneous thoughts to close out this chapter:

> **1.** It's very unusual for a player who has flopped two pair to check on both the flop and the turn. A player would usually bet to protect his hand. The practical application of this is that if a full house is possible on the river, the player usually does not have it if he checked on both the flop and the turn. Often, he is encouraged by the fact that you also checked and now he is trying to represent a full house. You should almost always call, and if you're really courageous, raise him. You'll often win the pot right there.

> **2.** If you flop a set and then run off a pair, your full house will be good 98 percent of the time. You have to be careful when the pair that comes on the turn and river is aces, kings or queens. Here's an example: You have Q♣ 10♦ and the flop is Q♦ 10♥ 10♠. The turn and river are A♥ A♠. Anyone holding A♣ 10♦ hit perfect-perfect to beat you. Rare, but it happens.

SUMMARY

It's impossible to tell you how to play every hand under all circumstances but a thorough understanding of the theory of poker will be a good guide for you. First, determine what your objective is, and then determine how best to accomplish it. You have many tools at your disposal—checking, betting, calling, check-raising, slowplaying, giving false tells—but the quality of your decision-making should be the overall deciding factor in your success in this game.

12

SHORT-HANDED GAMES

The most distinguishing feature of a short-handed game is the fact that much weaker hands than average will win the pots. It is statistically more likely that you can deal out a premium hand like A♦ K♠, K♣ Q♣ or J♠ J♥ in ten hands, than you can in just five hands. If you've never played in a short-handed game before and would like to have a feel for what it's like, try this simple exercise:

Using a deck of cards, deal out ten hold'em hands on the table in front of you. Deal out two rows of hands with five hands in each row. It might look like this:

10♠	8♣	9♠	7♦	A♣
2♥	3♦	Q♠	5♣	7♥
2♠	10♦	5♥	K♠	J♥
A♥	Q♣	8♦	J♦	4♦

Now put out cards for the flop, turn and river. Let's use this board: J♣ 4♠ 8♠ 3♣ K♥. The winning hand in this example is the K♠ J♦, but that is when you have ten hands to choose from. If you were to choose the winning hand from only the top row, it would be the 8♣ 3♦, a hand that is obviously inferior (heads-up before the flop) to K♠ J♦. The operative principle here is that as you have a greater number of hands from which to choose, the better the winning hand will be.

So, as there are more and more players dealt in at the beginning of the hand, the better the hand it will take to win if there is a showdown at the end. Conversely, as there are fewer and fewer players dealt in the hand, the weaker the winning hands will be at the showdown (if the hand gets that far). This is the essence of understanding how to play in a short-handed game. It calls for some pretty serious and drastic strategy changes on your part. Here is a list of things that you need to know about playing in a short-handed game:

1. Adapt to the Game

Remember that winning at poker requires skillful play. You must be willing and able to adapt to changing circumstances and conditions, one of which might be a short-handed game. Theoretically, poker is a perfectly balanced game. For every strategy, there is a correct counter-strategy. For every weakness that a player has, there's a way to take advantage of it. And there's a way to take advantage of an opponent's strengths also.

If you're going to be a poker player in the true sense of the term, you should not avoid a game solely because there aren't enough players in the game. You will have many, many games in your future that will be short-handed and they represent a potential goldmine for you if you know how to adjust to the conditions. In short, your attitude toward these games is probably the major contributing factor to your success or failure.

2. Pay Attention During the Game

Often, a game will change from a full game to a short-handed game without anyone realizing it or mentioning it at the table. It's been my experience that a game takes on the major characteristics of a short-handed game when there are six or fewer players being dealt in at the beginning of the hand. This is when the short-handed strategies become more effective. Also, when you realize that the game has become short-handed, do not announce it for all to hear. Poker is a game of concealed information and you should not educate your opponents at the table, even though certain facts are out there in the open for all to see.

3. Ask for Rake Breaks and a Single Blind

Ask the house for a rake break and a single blind if you're playing in a casino poker room. This is critical because the pots are smaller in a short-handed game and the $2 or $3 that the house takes out of every pot represents a larger percentage of the pot.

4. Think About Various Factors Before Quitting Play

Your decision regarding when to quit the game takes on a different perspective. You have to think about various factors. You have to consider what time of day it is. The game might be short-handed because it's six o'clock in the morning, but you know if you wait another hour or so the regular day players will be coming in to fill up the table. Is there another, better game to go to? Or is it 3 a.m. and there's no money on the table and there's no other game to go to? Think ahead. The game will fill up, but is it worth waiting around for?

5. Big Cards Become Stronger

Big cards in the pocket do not have to improve as much to win in a short-handed game. A♦ K♠ will win more often without improving. A river card that could make a possible flush or straight is not as likely to hurt you as much as it would in a full game. Scare cards are more likely to be just that. If you hold A♥ J♠ and get another jack on the flop to make top pair with top kicker, a king or queen on the river is not as likely to hurt you since you'll be facing fewer players.

6. Forget That You Are Suited

If you are, you will almost never get the right odds to draw to a straight or a flush in a short-handed game. You should look at being suited as an added bonus those few times you make a flush using both hole cards. My previous advice about limping in with A♥ K♥ and the like does not apply since you're not primarily drawing to the flush. You should rely on the high ranks of your cards to win the hand. Because of that, you should usually raise preflop with Big Slick and other big hands.

The value of big cards goes up while the value of drawing cards in the pocket (such as 7♦ 9♦) goes down in a short-handed game.

7. Play More Aggressively

You should usually play more aggressively before and on the flop when you have big cards. Your raises will further reduce the field, which will in turn further increase your chance of having the best hand at the end. Because it's correct for you to play more hands and raise more often, it's also correct for everyone else to play that way. This means that more players will be doing more raising with weaker hands than average, and that almost every hand will be an exercise in blind-stealing. The problem comes in knowing when your opponents are playing a short-handed strategy or when they have a legitimately strong hand. It's difficult to give a definitive answer on this subject, but your best guides are to know your players and to stick to a somewhat solid strategy yourself.

In those instances where you can't decide if a raise means a steal or a good hand, you should usually consider it to be a steal. You will be wrong once in a while, but I think that's the best way to play it in the long run.

8. You Do Not Always Need the Nuts to Win

Often, just an ace-high or a pair will win the hand. You can bet weaker hands with more confidence, especially if it would be a good hand in a full game. A raise on the flop is more likely to be intended to protect a weaker hand than it would in a full game.

For example, you hold J♠ 10♦ and the flop is J♥ 6♥ 5♣. In a full game, you might check and fold this hand if there's a bet with a large field. But in a short-handed game, you probably have the best hand at this point, and a raise from you will help protect it and insure that fewer players are chasing you down with straight and flush draws.

9. Play a Straightforward Game

Fancy plays are less likely to be successful in a typical short-handed low-limit game. Forget about check-raising, slowplaying, and other attempts at deception. Don't be afraid to bet and raise with your good hands because the other players will assume that you don't have that great a hand. They will think you are playing your standard short-handed game, which does entail a lot of betting and raising. In other words, the fact that the game is short-handed will disguise the fact that you're betting for value, when you do have a fantastic hand.

10. Be Aware of Loose and Wild Players

Be aware of those times when a ten-handed game is full of loose, wild players playing and betting every hand. This is a common situation in a weekend hold'em game in a casino poker room. As more and more players drop out of the game, the more correct this loose and wild strategy becomes. These players are unwittingly playing a good short-handed game, but this strength does not help them until the game actually becomes short-handed.

11. Adjust Your Strategies

There are a few specific strategy changes that you can make in a short-handed game. You can give free cards more often. With fewer players in the game, a free card is less likely to hurt you. You can bet middle and bottom pairs more, because it will actually be the best hand more often than in a full game. You can bet your draws more often, especially if you're holding the big cards in the draw. You can semibluff more often, because what would be a semibluff in a full game is often actually a bet for value in a short-handed game.

12. Other Considerations

The fewer the number of players there are in the game, the more small advantages are worth to you. There are fewer of you to split all of that money that the drunk in the game is losing. Early position is less vulnerable because there are fewer players to raise behind you. If you're playing tight, you'll be more successful because you won't have to wait as long for the blinds to come around. And if you're the best player in the game, you'll get to play more hands per hour because of that.

There are no hard-and-fast rules about how to play in a short-handed game. You have to be flexible and be able to adjust to your opponents' styles of play. Put yourself in their shoes and realize that it would be correct for them to play more hands and do more raising, especially before the flop.

SHORT-HANDED GAMES

Whenever I'm in a short-handed game and I hear one player continually complaining about all the raising, I know that I'm in a game with someone who really doesn't understand the game. Your best guide is experience. You shouldn't pass up a good, profitable game just because it might be short-handed. Being able to play short-handed games will make you a better player in the long run.

13

HOLD'EM ODDS

ODDS FOR YOUR HOLE CARDS

There are exactly 1,326 different ways you can be dealt any two cards in the deck. There are six ways to have a pair because any card can be matched with any one of the other three of its rank like this: ♣ ♦, ♣ ♥, ♣ ♠, ♦ ♥, ♦ ♠, and ♥ ♠. Any two cards that are not a pair can come in these combinations: ♣ ♣, ♣ ♦, ♣ ♥, ♣ ♠, ♦ ♣, ♦ ♦, ♦ ♥, ♦ ♠, ♥ ♣, ♥ ♦, ♥ ♥, ♥ ♠, ♠ ♣, ♠ ♦, ♠ ♥ and ♠ ♠. Four of these combinations are suited.

If you consider the fact that J♥ 7♦ and J♣ 7♠ are the same hand because they are not suited, then there are only 169 ways to be dealt two cards. All 169 hands are printed in descending order on the following page.

Odds That You'll Be Dealt These Hands	
A-A	220-1
Any pair in the pocket	16-1
A-K (suited)	331-1
A-K (not suited)	110-1
Any two suited cards	3.25-1
Any pair or an ace	3.91-1
At least one ace	5.7-1
Any 2 suited and connected	26.6-1

All 169 Possible Two-card Hold'em Hands
s = Suited

1.	AA	43.	Q5s	85.	62s	127.	J8
2.	KK	44.	Q4s	86.	54s	128.	J7
3.	QQ	45.	Q3s	87.	53s	129.	J6
4.	JJ	46.	Q2s	88.	52s	130.	J5
5.	TT	47.	JTs	89.	43s	131.	J4
6.	99	48.	J9s	90.	42s	132.	J3
7.	88	49.	J8s	91.	32s	133.	J2
8.	77	50.	J7s	92.	AK	134.	T9
9.	66	51.	J6s	93.	AQ	135.	T8
10.	55	52.	J5s	94.	AJ	136.	T7
11.	44	53.	J4s	95.	AT	137.	T6
12.	33	54.	J3s	96.	A9	138.	T5
13.	22	55.	J2s	97.	A8	139.	T4
14.	AKs	56.	T9s	98.	A7	140.	T3
15.	AQs	57.	T8s	99.	A6	141.	T2
16.	AJs	58.	T7s	100.	A5	142.	98
17.	ATs	59.	T6s	101.	A4	143.	97
18.	A9s	60.	T5s	102.	A3	144.	96
19.	A8s	61.	T4s	103.	A2	145.	95
20.	A7s	62.	T3s	104.	KQ	146.	94
21.	A6s	63.	T2s	105.	KJ	147.	93
22.	A5s	64.	98s	106.	KT	148.	92
23.	A4s	65.	97s	107.	K9	149.	87
24.	A3s	66.	96s	108.	K8	150.	86
25.	A2s	67.	95s	109.	K7	151.	85
26.	KQs	68.	94s	110.	K6	152.	84
27.	KJs	69.	93s	111.	K5	153.	83
28.	KTs	70.	92s	112.	K4	154.	82
29.	K9s	71.	87s	113.	K3	155.	76
30.	K8s	72.	86s	114.	K2	156.	75
31.	K7s	73.	85s	115.	QJ	157.	74
32.	K6s	74.	84s	116.	QT	158.	73
33.	K5s	75.	83s	117.	Q9	159.	72
34.	K4s	76.	82s	118.	Q8	160.	65
35.	K3s	77.	76s	119.	Q7	161.	64
36.	K2s	78.	75s	120.	Q6	162.	63
37.	QJs	79.	74s	121.	Q5	163.	62
38.	QTs	80.	73s	122.	Q4	164.	54
39.	Q9s	81.	72s	123.	Q3	165.	53
40.	Q8s	82.	65s	124.	Q2	166.	52
41.	Q7s	83.	64s	125.	JT	167.	43
42.	Q6s	84.	63s	126.	J9	169.	32

Preflop Percentages That No One Else Holds These Hands	
An ace (10-handed game)	13.3%
An ace if you do (10-handed)	25.3%
An ace if you don't (10-handed game)	15.6%
An ace (5-handed game)	41.3%
An ace if you do (5-handed game)	58.6%
An ace if you don't (5-handed game)	48.6%

ODDS THAT SOMEONE HOLDS A BETTER HAND THAN YOU DO PREFLOP

Because of the community card nature of the game and the fact that high cards beat low cards, it is critical that your hole cards be better than your opponent's, on average. If you have Q♥ J♠ and your opponent has A♣ Q♦, then you might as well be playing with only your J♠ because pairing your queen doesn't help you at all (not counting straight draws).

Holding a common card with an opponent whose second card is higher than yours makes you about a 4-1 underdog before the flop. In the example above, if you both miss, he wins with his ace high. If you both pair your queens, he wins with his ace kicker. For easier reading, odds that are less than 1 to 1 are expressed as a percentage (%) from this point on.

Odds That Someone Holds a Better Hand Than You Do Preflop

You hold	Odds that someone else holds	Number of players dealt in the hand		
		8	9	10
K♣ K♦	A♥ A♠	24.6-1	21.8-1	19.5-1
A♦ K♥	A♠ A♥, K♠ K♣	24.8-1	21.9-1	19.7-1
Q♦ Q♣	A♥ A♠, K♣ K♠	12.0-1	10.6-1	9.5-1
J♣ J♦	A♣ A♦, K♥ K♠, Q♦ Q♥	7.9-1	6.9-1	6.2-1
T♠ T♥	A♣ A♦, K♦ K♥, Q♠ Q♣, J♥ J♦	5.8-1	5.1-1	4.5-1
A♥ Q♠	A♣ A♦, K♥ K♠, A♥ K♦, Q♣ Q♠	5.7-1	5.0-1	4.4-1
9♥ 9♦	A♣ A♦, K♥ K♠, Q♦ Q♥, J♠ J♣, T♣ T♦	4.5-1	4.0-1	3.5-1
K♠ Q♥	A♣ A♦, K♥ K♠, Q♦ Q♥, A♣ K♦, A♦ Q♠	3.6-1	3.1-1	2.7-1
A♥ J♠	A♣ A♦, K♥ K♠, Q♦ Q♥, J♠ J♣, A♦ K♣, A♥ Q♣	3.0-1	2.6-1	2.3-1
K♦ J♠	A♣ A♦, K♥ K♠, Q♠ Q♥, J♦ J♣, A♦ K♥, A♣ J♥, K♠ Q♥	2.2-1	1.9-1	1.7-1
A♥ T♦	A♣ A♦, K♥ K♠, Q♦ Q♥, J♠ J♣, T♥ T♣, A♦ K♥, A♠ Q♣, A♥ J♣	1.9-1	1.7-1	1.4-1
Q♥ J♣	A♣ A♦, K♥ K♠, Q♦ Q♥, J♣ J♠, A♦ Q♣, A♠ J♣, K♥ Q♥, K♦ J♣	1.7-1	1.5-1	1.3-1
K♠ T♦	A♣ A♦, K♥ K♠, Q♦ Q♥, J♣ J♥, T♥ T♦, A♥ K♣, A♠ T♣, K♥ Q♦, K♣ J♠	1.5-1	1.3-1	1.1-1
A♦ 9♥	A♣ A♦, K♥ K♠, Q♦ Q♥, J♣ J♠, T♥ T♦, 9♠ 9♦, A♣ K♦, A♥ Q♠, A♣ J♠, A♥ T♦	1.4-1	1.2-1	50.2%
Q♠ T♥	A♣ A♦, K♥ K♠, Q♣ Q♠, J♦ J♥, T♠ T♦, A♥ Q♦, A♣ T♠, K♥ Q♦, K♠ T♦, Q♣ J♥	1.2-1	1.0-1	52.9%
K♥ 9♦	A♣ A♦, K♥ K♠, Q♦ Q♥, J♠ J♣, T♦ T♥, 9♥ 9♦, A♠ K♥, A♥ 9♦, K♦ Q♠, K♣ J♦, K♥ T♠	1.1-1	51.5%	55.5%

THE TOP 40 HOLD'EM HANDS, BASED ON EARNING POWER

There's been a lot of speculation about which hand is better than another and exactly how they should be ranked. To make this determination, you have to consider how high or low the pocket cards are, if they're suited or not, can they make a straight, can they make the nuts, do they fare better against a large field or against one opponent, and can they win without much improvement.

When all of these factors are combined, they determine the ultimate consideration; how profitable is the hand for you? How much money does the hand make?

Recent computer analysis suggests that of all 169 possible hold'em hands, the top 40 hands, in descending order, go like this:

The Top 40 Hold'em Hands
Based on Earning Power

Rank	Hand	% Chance or Better*	Odds-to-1 or Better**
1	A-A	0.45	220.00
2	K-K	0.90	109.50
3	Q-Q	1.36	72.67
4	J-J	1.81	54.25
5	A-Ks	2.11	46.36
6	10-10	2.56	38.00
7	A-K	3.02	32.15
8	A-Qs	3.77	25.52
9	K-Qs	4.07	23.56
10	A-Js	4.37	21.86
11	A-10s	4.68	20.39
12	A-Q	5.58	16.92
13	9-9	6.03	15.58
14	K-Js	6.33	14.79
15	K-Q	7.24	12.81
16	K-10s	7.54	12.26
17	A-9s	7.84	11.75
18	A-J	8.75	10.43
19	8-8	9.20	9.87
20	Q-Js	9.50	9.52
21	K-J	10.41	8.61
22	A-8s	10.71	8.34
23	A-10	11.61	7.61
24	Q-10s	11.92	7.39
25	K-9s	12.22	7.19
26	J-10s	12.52	6.99
27	A-5s	12.82	6.80
28	A-4s	13.12	6.62
29	Q-J	14.03	6.13
30	A-7s	14.33	5.98
31	K-8s	14.63	5.84
32	K-10	15.54	5.44
33	Q-9s	15.84	5.31
34	A-3s	16.14	5.20
35	A-6s	16.44	5.08
36	A-2s	16.74	4.97
37	Q-10	17.65	4.67
38	K-7s	17.95	4.57
39	7-7	18.40	4.43
40	J-9s	18.70	4.35

The "s" after a hand indicates that the two pocket cards are suited. If there is no "s," then the cards are no t suited.

* This is the percent chance that you will be dealt this hand or any one of the hands above it on the list.

** This is the percent column converted to odds. For example, your chance of being dealt K-Q suited or any of the eight hands above it is 4.07 percent, converted to odds is 23.56-1.

OVERCARDS

An **overcard** is a card on the flop that is higher than the highest card in your hand. It represents the threat that it has paired one of your opponent's hole cards.

If you have 10♣ 10♥, then you definitely would not like a flop like K♥ 8♦ 6♠ against six players. Any player betting in front of you is representing at least a pair of kings. Whether or not he actually has a king is for you to figure out and it usually means you'll have to fold your hand, even if you sometimes actually have the best hand at that point.

You must have an ace in the pocket to not have to worry about an overcard, and that's going to happen only 14.9 percent of the time. The "X" in the following table represents any card lower than the one named.

Percent Chance That You Will Flop an Overcard

You Hold	Number of Overcards 0	1	2	3	An Overcard 1/More	& No Set if Paired
K♣ K♦ or KX	77.449	21.122	1.408	0.020	22.550	11.67
Q♦ Q♥ or QX	58.571	35.143	6.000	0.286	41.429	31.12
J♥ J♠ or JX	43.041	43.041	12.796	1.122	56.959	46.96
10♠ 10♣ or TX	30.531	45.796	20.816	2.875	69.487	59.57
9♣ 9♦ or 9X	20.714	44.388	29.082	5.816	79.286	69.30
8♦ 8♥ or 8X	13.265	39.796	36.612	10.327	86.735	76.54
7♥ 7♠ or 7X	7.857	33.000	42.429	16.714	92.143	81.65
6♠ 6♣ or 6X	4.163	24.980	45.551	25.306	95.837	85.01
5♣ 5♦ or 5X	1.857	16.714	45.000	36.429	98.143	86.97
4♦ 4♥ or 4X	0.612	9.184	39.796	50.408	99.388	87.92
3♥ 3♠ or 3X	0.102	3.367	28.959	67.571	99.898	88.22
2♠ 2♣	impossible	0.245	11.510	88.245	100.000	88.24

None, one, two and three means the chance of having exactly that many overcards come on the flop. For example, if you hold Q♥ Q♣, there will be exactly two overcards (aces or kings) on the flop 6.0 percent of the time. The *One or More* column is simply the total of the one, two and three columns.

Note that there is barely any difference between a pair of deuces and a pair of eights in the pocket when it comes to flopping an overcard. A jack in the pocket is the median hand for flopping an overcard. You'll get one or more overcards 57 percent of the time, while you'll flop an overcard to a queen only 41 percent of the time. That is why in a multiway pot I do not raise preflop with J♥ J♦ in the pocket. I know I'll get an overcard over half the time, so I see the flop as cheaply as possible.

The column on the far right shows the odds of getting at least one overcard and not flopping a set when you hold a pair in the pocket. In other words, it gives the odds that you won't like the flop.

BASIC ODDS FOR THE FLOP

The following table lists all of the 169 possible starting hands and the odds of making specific hands on the flop. There are a few things you should be aware of to help you make sense of the statistics:

A. There are exactly 19,600 ways to flop three cards given your two hold cards. So, the odds of flopping any three exact cards you specify are 19,599 to 1.

B. When your hand is a pair, you will flop a full house .98 percent of the time. However, one-fourth of the time it will be with a set on the board and your full house will not be very well disguised. For example, if you hold 8♦ 8♥, you will make your full house by flopping an 8 with a pair only .7125 percent of the time. That's three-fourths of .98 percent; the total odds of making any full house.

C. When your hand is not a pair, you will flop three of

a kind 1.57 percent of the time. However, one-seventh of these will be with the three of a kind on the board. So, when you hold something like K♦ J♠, you will get two kings or two jacks on the flop 1.347 percent of the time (6/7ths of 1.571 percent).

D. When your hand is not a pair, you will flop two pair 4.041 percent of the time, but exactly one-half of these will be with one of the pairs on the board. That means that your two pair on the flop will be concealed only half of the time.

E. When your hand is not a pair, you will flop one pair 40.408 percent of the time. However, one-third of these pairs will be on the board and not pair one of your hole cards. That means you will flop one of your hole cards 26.939 percent of the time.

F. The chance of flopping a four flush when you are suited is 10.944 percent. The chance of flopping a four flush when you are not suited is 2.245 percent.

G. Any time you are suited and connected, i.e., you hold 8♥ 7♥, you will flop both a straight and a flush draw 3.352 percent of the time.

H. The "s" after a hand in the following chart means suited. A-Ks means A-K suited. A-K without an "s" means the hand is not suited.

Basic Odds for the Flop In Percentages - A

You Hold	ST Flush	4 of Kind	Full House	Flush	Straight	3 of Kind	Two Pair	One Pair	4-STRT
A♣ A♦	—	.245	.980	—	—	10.776	16.163	71.837	2.612
K♦ K♥	—	.245	.980	—	—	10.776	16.163	71.837	2.612
Q♥ Q♠	—	.245	.980	—	—	10.776	16.163	71.837	2.612
J♠ J♣	—	.245	.980	—	—	10.776	16.163	71.837	2.612
10♣ 10♦	—	.245	.980	—	—	10.776	16.163	71.837	2.612
9♦ 9♥	—	.245	.980	—	—	10.776	16.163	71.837	2.612
8♥ 8♠	—	.245	.980	—	—	10.776	16.163	71.837	2.612
7♠ 7♣	—	.245	.980	—	—	10.776	16.163	71.837	2.612
6♣ 6♦	—	.245	.980	—	—	10.776	16.163	71.837	2.612
5♦ 5♥	—	.245	.980	—	—	10.776	16.163	71.837	2.612
4♥ 4♠	—	.245	.980	—	—	10.776	16.163	71.837	2.612
3♠ 3♣	—	.245	.980	—	—	10.776	16.163	71.837	2.612
2♣ 2♦	—	.245	.980	—	—	10.776	16.163	71.837	2.612
AKs	.005	.010	.092	.837	.321	1.571	4.041	40.408	11.204
AK	—	.010	.092	—	.327	1.571	4.041	40.408	11.347
AQs	.005	.010	.092	.837	.321	1.571	4.041	40.408	11.847
AQ	—	.010	.092	—	.327	1.571	4.041	40.408	12.000
AJs	.005	.010	.092	.837	.321	1.571	4.041	40.408	12.811
AJ	—	.010	.092	—	.327	1.571	4.041	40.408	12.980
ATs	.005	.010	.092	.837	.321	1.571	4.041	40.408	13.776
AT	—	.010	.092	—	.327	1.571	4.041	40.408	13.959
A9s	—	.010	.092	.837	—	1.571	4.041	40.408	6.429
A9	—	.010	.092	—	—	1.571	4.041	40.408	6.531
A8s	—	.010	.092	.842	—	1.571	4.041	40.408	7.393
A8	—	.010	.092	—	—	1.571	4.041	40.408	7.510
A7s	—	.010	.092	.842	—	1.571	4.041	40.408	7.393
A7	—	.010	.092	—	—	1.571	4.041	40.408	7.510
A6s	—	.010	.092	.842	—	1.571	4.041	40.408	6.429
A6	—	.010	.092	—	—	1.571	4.041	40.408	6.531
A5s	.005	.010	.092	.837	.321	1.571	4.041	40.408	13.776
A5	—	.010	.092	—	.327	1.571	4.041	40.408	13.959
A4s	.005	.010	.092	.837	.321	1.571	4.041	40.408	12.811
A4	—	.010	.092	—	.327	1.571	4.041	40.408	12.980
A3s	.005	.010	.092	.837	.321	1.571	4.041	40.408	11.847
A3	—	.010	.092	—	.327	1.571	4.041	40.408	12.000
A2s	.005	.010	.092	.837	.321	1.571	4.041	40.408	11.204
A2	—	.010	.092	—	.327	1.571	4.041	40.408	11.347
KQs	.010	.010	.092	.832	.643	1.571	4.041	40.408	15.566
KQ	—	.010	.092	—	.653	1.571	4.041	40.408	15.755
KJs	.010	.010	.092	.832	.643	1.571	4.041	40.408	16.209
KJ	—	.010	.092	—	.653	1.571	4.041	40.408	16.408
KTs	.010	.010	.092	.832	.643	1.571	4.041	40.408	17.173
KT	—	.010	.092	—	.653	1.571	4.041	40.408	17.388
K9s	.005	.010	.092	.837	.321	1.571	4.041	40.408	12.490

Basic Odds for the Flop In Percentages - B

You Hold	ST Flush	4 of Kind	Full House	Flush	Straight	3 of Kind	Two Pair	One Pair	4-STRT
K9	—	.010	.092	—	.327	1.571	4.041	40.408	12.653
K8s	—	.010	.092	.842	—	1.571	4.041	40.408	6.107
K8	—	.010	.092	—	—	1.571	4.041	40.408	6.204
K7s	—	.010	.092	.842	—	1.571	4.041	40.408	7.071
K7	—	.010	.092	—	—	1.571	4.041	40.408	7.184
K6s	—	.010	.092	.842	—	1.571	4.041	40.408	7.393
K6	—	.010	.092	—	—	1.571	4.041	40.408	7.510
K5s	—	.010	.092	.837	—	1.571	4.041	40.408	7.393
K5	—	.010	.092	—	—	1.571	4.041	40.408	7.510
K4s	—	.010	.092	.842	—	1.571	4.041	40.408	6.429
K4	—	.010	.092	—	—	1.571	4.041	40.408	6.531
K3s	—	.010	.092	.842	—	1.571	4.041	40.408	5.464
K3	—	.010	.092	—	—	1.571	4.041	40.408	5.551
K2s	—	.101	.092	.842	—	1.571	4.041	40.408	4.500
K2	—	.010	.092	—	—	1.571	4.041	40.408	4.571
QJs	.015	.010	.092	.827	.964	1.571	4.041	40.408	20.893
QJ	—	.010	.092	—	.980	1.571	4.041	40.408	21.143
QTs	.015	.010	.092	.827	.964	1.571	4.041	40.408	21.356
QT	—	.010	.021	—	.980	1.571	4.041	40.408	21.796
Q9s	.010	.010	.092	.832	.643	1.571	4.041	40.408	17.173
Q9	—	.010	.092	—	.653	1.571	4.041	40.408	17.388
Q8s	.005	.010	.092	.837	.321	1.571	4.041	40.408	13.133
Q8	—	.010	.092	—	.327	1.571	4.041	40.408	13.306
Q7s	—	.010	.092	.842	—	1.571	4.041	40.408	7.071
Q7	—	.010	.092	—	—	1.571	4.041	40.408	7.184
Q6s	—	.010	.092	.842	—	1.571	4.041	40.408	8.036
Q6	—	.010	.092	—	—	1.571	4.041	40.408	8.163
Q5s	—	.010	.092	.842	—	1.571	4.041	40.408	8.357
Q5	—	.010	.092	—	—	1.571	4.041	40.408	8.490
Q4s	—	.010	.092	.842	—	1.571	4.041	40.408	7.393
Q4	—	.010	.092	—	—	1.571	4.041	40.408	7.510
Q3s	—	.010	.092	.842	—	1.571	4.041	40.408	6.429
Q3	—	.010	.092	—	—	1.571	4.041	40.408	6.531
Q2s	—	.010	.092	.842	—	1.571	4.041	40.408	5.464
Q2	—	.010	.092	—	—	1.571	4.041	40.408	5.551
JTs	.020	.010	.092	.821	1.286	1.571	4.041	40.408	26.219
JT	—	.010	.092	—	1.306	1.571	4.041	40.408	25.531
J9s	.015	.010	.092	.837	.064	1.571	4.041	40.408	21.536
J9	—	.010	.092	—	.980	1.571	4.041	40.408	21.796
J8s	.005	.010	.092	.832	.643	1.571	4.041	40.408	17.816
J8	—	.010	.092	—	.653	1.571	4.041	40.408	18.041
J7s	.005	.010	.092	.837	.321	1.571	4.041	40.408	14.097
J7	—	.010	.092	—	.327	1.571	4.041	40.408	14.286
J6s	—	.010	.092	.842	—	1.571	4.041	40.408	8.036

Basic Odds For the Flop In Percentages - C

You Hold	ST Flush	4 of Kind	Full House	Flush	Straight	3 of Kind	Two Pair	One Pair	4-STRT
J6	—	.010	.092	—	—	1.571	4.041	40.408	8.163
J5s	—	.010	.092	.842	—	1.571	4.041	40.408	9.000
J5	—	.010	.092	—	—	1.571	4.041	40.408	9.143
J4s	—	.010	.092	.842	—	1.571	4.041	40.408	8.357
J4	—	.010	.092	—	—	1.571	4.041	40.408	8.490
J3s	—	.010	.092	.842	—	1.571	4.041	40.408	7.393
J3	—	.010	.092	—	—	1.571	4.041	40.408	7.510
J2s	—	.010	.092	.842	—	1.571	4.041	40.408	6.429
J2	—	.010	.092	—	—	1.571	4.041	40.408	6.531
T9s	.020	.010	.092	.821	1.286	1.571	4.041	40.408	26.219
T9	—	.010	.092	—	1.306	1.571	4.041	40.408	26.531
T8s	.015	.010	.092	.827	.964	1.571	4.041	40.408	22.179
T8	—	.010	.092	—	.980	1.571	4.041	40.408	22.449
T7s	.010	.010	.092	.832	.643	1.571	4.041	40.408	18.871
T7	—	.010	.092	—	.653	1.571	4.041	40.408	19.020
T6s	—	.010	.092	.837	—	1.571	4.041	40.408	15.061
T6	—	.010	.092	—	.327	1.571	4.041	40.408	15.265
T5s	—	.010	.092	.842	—	1.571	4.041	40.408	9.000
T5	—	.010	.092	—	—	1.571	4.041	40.408	9.143
T4s	—	.010	.092	.842	—	1.571	4.041	40.408	9.000
T4	—	.010	.092	—	—	1.571	4.041	40.408	9.143
T3s	—	.010	.092	.842	—	1.571	4.041	40.408	8.357
T3	—	.010	.092	—	—	1.571	4.041	40.408	8.490
T2s	—	.010	.092	.842	—	1.571	4.041	40.408	7.393
T2	—	.010	.092	—	—	1.571	4.041	40.408	7.510
98s	.020	.010	.092	.821	1.286	1.571	4.041	40.408	26.219
98	—	.010	.092	—	1.306	1.571	4.041	40.408	25.531
97s	.015	.010	.092	.827	.964	1.571	4.041	40.408	22.179
97	—	.010	.092	—	.980	1.571	4.041	40.408	22.449
96s	.010	.010	.092	.832	.643	1.571	4.041	40.408	18.781
96	—	.010	.092	—	.653	1.571	4.041	40.408	19.020
95s	.005	.010	.092	.842	.321	1.571	4.041	40.408	15.061
95	—	.010	.092	—	.327	1.571	4.041	40.408	15.265
94s	—	.010	.092	.842	—	1.571	4.041	40.408	8.036
94	—	.010	.092	—	—	1.571	4.041	40.408	8.163
93s	—	.010	.092	.842	—	1.571	4.041	40.408	8.036
93	—	.010	.092	—	—	1.571	4.041	40.408	8.163
92s	—	.010	.092	.842	—	1.571	4.041	40.408	7.393
92	—	.010	.092	—	—	1.571	4.041	40.408	7.510
87s	.020	.010	.092	.821	1.286	1.571	4.041	40.408	26.219
87	—	.010	.092	—	1.306	1.571	4.041	40.408	25.531
86s	.015	.010	.092	.827	.964	1.571	4.041	40.408	22.179
86	—	.010	.092	—	.980	1.571	4.041	40.408	22.449

Basic Odds For the Flop In Percentages - D

You Hold	ST Flush	4 of Kind	Full House	Flush	Straight	3 of Kind	Two Pair	One Pair	4-STRT
85s	.010	.010	.092	.832	.643	1.571	4.041	40.408	18.781
85	—	.010	.092	—	.653	1.571	4.041	40.408	19.020
84s	.005	.010	.092	.837	.321	1.571	4.041	40.408	14.097
84	—	.010	.092	—	.327	1.571	4.041	40.408	14.286
83s	—	.010	.092	.842	—	1.571	4.041	40.408	7.071
83	—	.010	.092	—	—	1.571	4.041	40.408	7.184
82s	—	.010	.092	.842	—	1.571	4.041	40.408	7.071
82	—	.010	.092	—	—	1.571	4.041	40.408	7.184
76s	.020	.010	.092	.821	1.286	1.571	4.041	40.408	26.219
76	—	.010	.092	—	1.303	1.571	4.041	40.408	26.531
75s	.015	.010	.092	.827	.964	1.571	4.041	40.408	22.179
75	—	.010	.092	—	.980+	1.571	4.041	40.408	22.449
74s	.010	.010	.092	.832	.643	1.571	4.041	40.408	17.816
74	—	.010	.092	—	.653	1.571	4.041	40.408	18.041
73s	.005	.010	.092	.837	.321	1.571	4.041	40.408	13.133
73	—	.010	.092	—	.327	1.571	4.041	40.408	13.306
72s	—	.010	.092	.842	—	1.571	4.041	40.408	6.107
72	—	.010	.092	—	—	1.571	4.041	40.408	6.204
65s	.020	.010	.092	.821	1.286	1.571	4.041	40.408	26.219
65	—	.010	.092	—	1.306	1.571	4.041	40.408	26.531
64s	.015	.010	.092	.827	.964	1.571	4.041	40.408	21.536
64	—	.010	.092	—	.980	1.571	4.041	40.408	21.796
63s	.010	.010	.092	.832	.643	1.571	4.041	40.408	17.173
63	—	.010	.092	---	.653	1.571	4.041	40.408	17.388
62s	.005	.010	.092	.837	.321	1.571	4.041	40.408	12.490
62	—	.010	.092	—	.327	1.571	4.041	40.408	12.653
54s	.020	.010	.092	.821	1.286	1.571	4.041	40.408	26.219
54	—	.010	.092	—	1.306	1.571	4.041	40.408	26.531
53s	.015	.010	.092	.827	.964	1.571	4.041	40.408	21.536
53	—	.010	.092	—	.980	1.571	4.041	40.408	21.796
52s	.010	.010	.092	.832	.643	1.571	4.041	40.408	17.173
52	—	.010	.092	—	.653	1.571	4.041	40.408	17.388
43s	.015	.010	.092	.827	.964	1.571	4.041	40.408	20.893
43	—	.010	.092	—	.980	1.571	4.041	40.408	21.143
42s	.010	.010	.092	.832	.643	1.571	4.041	40.408	16.209
42	—	.010	.092	—	.653	1.571	4.041	40.408	16.408
32s	.010	.010	.092	.832	.643	1.571	4.041	40.408	16.566
32	—	.010	.092	—	.653	1.571	4.041	40.408	15.755

When you hold two cards in your hand and there are three cards on the flop, there will be 47 cards left in the deck that you have not seen. The fact that some of these 47 cards will have been dealt out to the other players and that some of these 47 cards will even be in the muck is of no consequence when it comes to computing your outs. The fact is that an unseen card that you may need to complete your hand has the same chance of coming on the turn or river regardless of how many players were dealt into the hand or how many of them have folded during the play of the hand.

For example, you hold A♥ 9♥ and the flop is K♥ 7♠ 3♥. You have nine outs with two cards to come to make your flush, giving you a 35.0 percent chance of making the flush by the end. If you miss on the turn, your chances then go down to 19.6 percent to make the flush with one card to come.

Drawing Odds From a Deck of 47 Unseen Cards

# of Outs	Cards to Come		Example
	2	**1**	
20	67.5%	43.5%	
19	65.0%	41.3%	
18	62.4%	39.1%	
17	59.8%	37.0%	
16	57.0%	34.8%	
15	54.1%	32.6%	Open-end straight flush draw
14	51.2%	30.4%	
13	48.1%	28.3%	
12	45.0%	26.1%	Flopped a 4 flush and pairing a hole card wins.
11	41.7%	23.9%	
10	38.4%	21.7%	You flopped a set and missed the FH on the turn.
9	35.0%	19.6%	You flopped a 4 flush
8	31.5%	17.4%	Open-end straight draw
7	27.8%	15.2%	You flopped a set, need to fill up.
6	24.1%	13.0%	
5	20.4%	10.9%	You hold A♣ K♦ and flopped an A or K.
4	16.5%	8.7%	Inside straight draw/you pair both hole cards.
3	12.5%	6.5%	You have 1 pair and need to hit your kicker.
2	8.4%	4.3%	You hold a pair and did not flop a set.
1	4.3%	2.2%	You need exactly one specific card to win.

How Pocket Pairs Fare When Everybody Plays to the End

No. of Players	AA	KK	QQ	JJ	TT	99	88	77	66	55	44	33	22
2	88	85	82	79	77	74	71	68	65	63	60	57	55
3	76	72	68	64	60	56	52	48	45	43	40	37	34
4	68	63	58	54	50	46	43	39	36	33	30	26	22
7	44	39	34	30	27	25	23	21	20	19	17	16	15
10	34	30	26	22	20	18	16	14	13	12	11	10	10

1. This table lists the percentage chance of winning against random hands when you hold the specified pair in the pocket against the specified number of opponents and everyone plays to the end.

2. You will flop a set 10.776 percent of the time but if you miss, you'll still make your set by the river an additional 8.4 percent of the time.

3. Remember, if someone else has A♥ A♠ in the pocket and you also have a pair in the pocket, if doesn't matter if your pair is K♦ K♥ or 2♣ 2♠. You still need to improve to win the hand.

The following charts give the percent chance that you will win the hand when you hold the specified cards against the specified number of players and you all play to the end. Although this situation does not exactly represent what actually happens in actual hold'em games, it does serve to illustrate the relative values of all the hands. For example, when you hold K♥ J♦, your winning percentages are 61 percent in a two-handed game, 43 percent in a three-handed game, 35 percent in a four-handed game, 21 percent in a seven-handed game and 15 percent in a ten-handed game.

Winning Percentages for Four (4) Players
(Add 3 percent for suited cards)

	K	Q	J	T	9	8	7	6	5	4	3	2
A	41	39	38	37	36	34	33	31	30	29	28	27
K	-	36	35	33	31	30	28	27	26	25	24	23
Q	-	-	34	32	30	28	26	25	24	23	22	20
J	-	-	-	30	28	26	25	23	33	21	20	19
T	-	-	-	-	27	25	24	22	21	20	19	18
9	-	-	-	-	-	23	22	21	20	19	18	17
8	-	-	-	-	-	-	22	21	19	18	17	16
7	-	-	-	-	-	-	-	21	19	18	17	16
6	-	-	-	-	-	-	-	-	19	18	17	16
5	-	-	-	-	-	-	-	-	-	18	16	15
4	-	-	-	-	-	-	-	-	-	-	16	15
3	-	-	-	-	-	-	-	-	-	-	-	14

Winning Percentages for Seven (7) Players

	K	Q	J	T	9	8	7	6	5	4	3	2
A	27	25	24	23	21	20	18	17	16	15	14	13
K	-	22	21	19	18	17	16	15	14	13	12	11
Q	-	-	20	18	16	15	24	23	22	10	9	9
J	-	-	-	17	15	18	13	11	10	9	9	8
T	-	-	-	-	14	13	12	11	10	9	9	8
9	-	-	-	-	-	12	11	10	9	8	8	7
8	-	-	-	-	-	-	11	10	9	8	8	7
7	-	-	-	-	-	-	-	10	9	8	8	7
6	-	-	-	-	-	-	-	-	9	8	8	7
5	-	-	-	-	-	-	-	-	-	8	7	6
4	-	-	-	-	-	-	-	-	-	-	7	6
3	-	-	-	-	-	-	-	-	-	-	-	6

Winning Percentages for Ten (10) Players

	K	Q	J	T	9	8	7	6	5	4	3	2
A	21	19	17	16	15	14	13	12	11	10	9	8
K	-	17	15	14	13	12	11	10	9	8	8	7
Q	-	-	14	13	11	10	9	9	8	8	7	7
J	-	-	-	11	10	10	9	8	8	7	7	6
T	-	-	-	-	10	9	8	8	7	7	6	6
9	-	-	-	-	-	9	8	7	7	6	6	5
8	-	-	-	-	-	-	8	7	7	6	5	5
7	-	-	-	-	-	-	-	7	6	5	5	4
6	-	-	-	-	-	-	-	-	6	5	4	4
5	-	-	-	-	-	-	-	-	-	5	4	3
4	-	-	-	-	-	-	-	-	-	-	4	3
3	-	-	-	-	-	-	-	-	-	-	-	

14
PERSONAL POKER RECORD BOOK

DATE	WHERE	LIMIT	HOURS PLAYED	WON/LOSS	PER HR	W/L TOTAL

15

HOLD'EM POKER TERMS

A-X Suited - An ace and another card of the same suit, for example, A♦7♦

Add-on - In a tournament, the last chips that you can buy and add to your stack before the rebuy period ends.

Advertise - To make an apparent bad play or loose play in order to convince your opponents that you are a bad player so that they will call you more often with worse hands in the future. The catch is that you will then always have a much better hand than they expect.

All in – To bet all your remaining chips in the middle of a hand.

Backdoor - When a player makes a hand he originally wasn't drawing to. For example, you have A♦ Q♦ with a 10♠ 8♦ 5♦ on the flop to make a four flush. The turn and river cards are K♣ and J♥ and you make the straight instead of the flush.

B & M - Stands for "bricks and mortar." Refers to poker rooms that actually exist in buildings as opposed to poker rooms that exist in cyberspace on the Internet.

Backdoor - Making a hand you weren't originally drawing to by getting perfect cards on the turn and river. For example, you hold A♥J♣ and the flop is Q♣ 7♣ 3♥, giving you a flush draw. When the turn card is the K♠ and the river is the 10♦, you just made a backdoor straight.

Backraise - A reraise from a player who originally called, but when it was raised, he decided to reraise.

Bad Beat - To be beat, especially when you flopped a great hand, by a player who made a longshot draw.

Bankroll - The money you have set aside to play poker with. This money should be mentally, if not actually physically, separated from other money used for non-playing expenses.

Bicycle - A 5-high straight: 5♠ 4♥ 3♥ 2♦ A♣.

Big Blind - The biggest of two blinds in a hold'em game; a mandatory bet posted by the player two places to the dealer's left.

Big Slick - Nickname for A-K

Blank - A card that is of no apparent help to any active players in a poker hand. Also **Rag**.

Bluff - To bet with what you suspect is the losing hand in an attempt to win the pot by forcing opponents to fold better hands rather than call that bet.

Board - The cards that are turned face up in hold'em and which belong to everybody; also called **community cards**.

Boxed Card - A card that is found to be accidentally turned face up in the deck as the hand is being dealt. It is treated as a blank piece of paper and is replaced with a new card after the deal is completed for that round.

Broadway - An ace-high straight: A♣ K♦ Q♠ J♥ 10♣.

Burn or Burn Card - The top card that is mucked by the dealer before turning the flop, turn and river cards. This is to protect everyone in the event that card is marked or somehow known to one player.

Button - In casino games, a round, plastic disc with the world "Dealer" printed on each side. It moves with each new deal to indicate who holds the dealer's position.

Buy-in - The amount of money that it costs to play in a ring game or tournament.

Calling Station - A player who calls way too often when folding or raising might be a better option.

Cards Speak - All casino hold'em games are played *cards speak*. Your poker hand is what it is regardless of how you call or miscall it. If you turn your hand face up, the dealer will call the hands and award the pot to the player who actually has the best hand.

Case Card - The last card of a particular rank that has not been seen or is otherwise believed to still be in the deck.

Change Gears - To change from loose play to tight play, tight to loose, conservative to aggressive, or aggressive to conservative.

Chasing - Calling with bad cards without the proper pot odds, in an attempt to improve.

Check-Raise - To check when it is your turn to bet and then to raise when a player bets after you have checked.

Chopping - When the two blinds agree to take their blind money back and end the hand right there after all players have folded around to the small blind. The two blinds do this to avoid paying a rake in what would be a heads-up pot. Also, to split a pot among winners.

Cold Call - To call a bet and a raise at once as opposed to calling one bet and then calling a later raise in the same round.

Community Cards - See **Board**

Dominated Hand - When two players have like hands, such as a pocket pair or an ace with another card, the lower pocket pair and the hand with the lower kicker to go with the ace are the dominated hands. Dominated hands are typically 4 to 1 underdogs heads-up before the flop.

Double Belly Buster - A straight draw in Texas hold'em where you have eight outs without having an open-end straight. For example, you hold 8♦ 6♦ and the board is 10♥ 7♠ 4♦ 3♠ with one card to come. A draw of a 5 or 9 will complete your straight, yet your straight draw is not open-ended.

Drawing Dead - Attempting to make a particular poker hand that, even if you make, is already beaten or cannot possibly win.

Ducks - Deuces. 2♥ 2♣ is a pair of ducks. Four ducks is knows as Huey, Duey, Louie and Uncle Donald.

End - See **River**

Early Position - The first third of players in a hold'em game to act on their hands.

End - The fifth, and final, card in hold'em. Also called the **River**.

Fifth Street - The river, or end card in hold'em.

Flop - The first three community cards placed face up by the dealer.

Flop a Set - To have a pair in the pocket and to flop one of them to make three of a kind.

Flush Card - A card of the suit that you need to complete a flush or pick up a flush draw, or a card that could give other players a flush.

Flush Draw - To have four cards to a flush with one or more cards to come.

Fourth Street - The fourth community card in hold'em. Also called the **turn**.

Free Card - A card received on a betting round without cost because everyone checked.

Freezeout Tournament - A tournament where you are allowed to make only your initial buy-in, with no rebuys or add-ons allowed.

Full - Refers to full houses. Your three-of-a-kind is what you're full of. J♥ J♦ J♣ 7♠ 7♥ is "jacks full of sevens."

Gutshot - A straight draw where only one exact rank of card will make the straight, as opposed to an open-end straight draw or a double belly buster where one of two different ranks of cards can complete your straight draw.

Heads-up - A hand of poker or a game where there are only two players.

Implied Odds – The ratio of money needed to stay active in a pot, expressed in odds, to the amount of money not yet in the pot, but which you believe will be there before the hand is over.

Kicker - The unmatched card that completes your five-card hand when you make a pair or better. For example, you hold A♥ J♠ and the board is J♥ 8♦ 8♣ 6♠ 3♥. Your hand is two pair, jacks and eights, with an ace kicker.

Kill Game - A game where the limits are doubled for the next hand only after the same player has won two consecutive hands.

Late Position - The last third of players in a game to have to act on their hands.

Little Blind - The smaller of the two blinds in hold'em, posted by the first player to the dealer's left before the cards are dealt.

Middle Position - The middle third of players in a game to act on their hands; to have approximately an equal number of players before and after you in the play of a hand.

Muck - To fold and throw you hand into the discard pile. The discard pile is also called the muck.

No-Limit - A game where you can bet any amount you have in the game at any time—up to the limit of what your opponents can match.

Nuts - The best possible hand in the game, given the cards on board.

Off-Broadway - A king-high straight: K♦ Q♣ J♦ 10♠ 9♣.

On the Button - In hold'em, to be in the dealer's position and therefore last to act throughout the play of the hand (excluding the preflop round).

Outs - The number of cards that will help your hand. For example, if you have a four flush in hearts, then there are nine hearts, or nine *outs* that will help your hand.

Overcall - To call a bet after another player has also called the bet.

Overcard- A hole card that is higher than any board card.

Overlay - Pot odds better than what is mathematically required to break even in the long run.

Overpair - A pair in your hand that is higher than any card on the board. Q♦Q♥ is an over pair if the flop is J♥ 9♦ 5♣.

Pocket Cards - The two private cards that you are dealt that no one else sees.

Pot-Limit - A game where you can bet any amount up to what is in the pot.

Pot Odds - The ratio of the amount of money that it costs to call a bet compared to how much money is already in the pot.

Rabbit Hunting - Asking the dealer to see what the next card or cards would have been when the hand is over prior to the river.

Rag - See **Blank**.

Rainbow Flop - A flop of three different suits.

Represent - To play your hand in such a way so as to convince everyone that you have a strong hand—except you don't.

River - The fifth, and last, community card in hold'em; also called the *end*.

Rock - A poker player who plays only premium starting hands, and whose playing style is very conservative and low risk.

Runner-Runner - To catch two successive cards, which make your hand on both the turn and the river.

Rush - A winning streak.

Satellite - A one-table tournament where the combined buy-in money is exactly the buy-in required for a larger tournament. For example, the buy-in for the WSOP main event is $10,000. A satellite for that event would be when ten players each pay $1,000 to compete for a winner-take-all tournament. The winner is then obligated to use that $10,000 to enter the big tournament.

Semibluffing - Betting with a hand that, if called, does not figure to be the best hand at the moment but has a reasonable chance to be the best hand by the end.

Set - Three of a kind that's made up of a pair in your hand and one on the board.

Sheriff - A player who calls bluffs with any hand at all just because he can't stand to see a player get away with bluffing.

Slowplay - To play your hand in a much weaker manner than the strength of the hand would normally call for in order to disguise its strength.

Steal - To raise on the first betting round for the sole purpose of winning just the blind or ante money.

Straddle - When the player on the immediate left of the big blind raises before he gets his cards, which gives him the last option on the initial betting round. (Only allowed in some games.)

Straight Draw - To have four cards to a straight with one or more cards to come.

Suited Connectors - Two consecutive cards of the same suit. For example, A♥ K♥, 8♦ 7♦ or 5♣ 4♣.

Tell - A clue that helps you figure out what poker hand an opponent has.

Turn - The fourth community card in hold'em.

Under the Gun – The first to act on a betting round.

Up - Used to indicate two pair. "Aces up" is two pair.

Wheel - See **Bicycle**.

Zero Board - A five-card board where the highest possible hand is exactly three of a kind.

Do You Have a Question for the Author?

I'd like to hear from you. Tell me what you liked about this book and, more importantly to me, what you didn't like about the book. Was this book of immediate, practical help to you? Do you have suggestions or ideas about how to improve future editions of this book? Do you have a question about how to play a particular hand that you would like my opinion on? Be specific and provide as much information as possible about the poker hand in question.

I'd be delighted to hear from you and I will answer every email. My personal email address is Kennolga@yahoo.com.

GREAT CARDOZA POKER BOOKS
ADD THESE TO YOUR LIBRARY - ORDER NOW!

DANIEL NEGREANU'S POWER HOLD'EM STRATEGY by Daniel Negreanu. This power-packed book on beating no-limit hold'em is one of the three most influential poker books ever written. Negreanu headlines a collection of young great players—Todd Brunson, David Williams. Erick Lindgren, Evelyn Ng and Paul Wasicka—who share their insider professional moves and winning secrets. You'll learn about short-handed and heads-up play, high-limit cash games, a powerful beginner's strategy to neutralize professional players, and how to mix up your play and bluff and win big pots. The centerpiece, however, is Negreanu's powerful and revolutionary small ball strategy. You'll learn how to play hold'em with cards you never would have played before—and with fantastic results. The preflop, flop, turn and river will never look the same again. A must-have! 520 pages, $34.95.

POKER WIZARDS by Warwick Dunnett. In the tradition of Super System, an exclusive collection of champions and superstars have been brought together to share their strategies, insights, and tactics for winning big money at poker, specifically no-limit hold'em tournaments. This is priceless advice from players who individually have each made millions of dollars in tournaments, and collectively, have won more than 20 WSOP bracelets, two WSOP main events, 100 major tournaments and $50 million in tournament winnings! Featuring Daniel Negreanu, Dan Harrington, Marcel Luske, Kathy Liebert, Mike Sexton, Mel Judah, Marc Salem, T.J Cloutier and Chris "Jesus" Ferguson. This must-read book is a goldmine for all serious players, aspiring pros, and future champions! 352 pgs, $19.95.

POKER TOURNAMENT FORMULA 2: Advanced Strategies for Big Money Tournaments by Arnold Snyder. Probably the greatest tournament poker book ever written, and the most controversial in the last decade, Snyder's revolutionary work debunks commonly (and falsely) held beliefs. Snyder reveals the power of chip utility—the real secret behind winning tournaments—and covers utility ranks, tournament structures, small- and long-ball strategies, patience factors, the impact of structures, crushing the Harringbots and other player types, tournament phases, and much more. Includes big sections on Tools, Strategies, and Tournament Phases. A must buy! 500 pages, $24.95.

OMAHA HIGH-LOW: How to Win at the Lower Limits by Shane Smith. Practical advice specifically targeted for the popular low-limit games you play every day in casinos and online will have you making money, and show you how to avoid losing situations and cards that can cost you a bundle—the dreaded second-nut draws, trap hands, and two-way second-best action. Smith's proven strategies are spiced with plenty of wit and wisdom. You'll learn the basics of play against the typical opponents you'll face in low-limit games—the no-fold'em players and the rocks—and get winning tactics, illustrated hands, and tournament tips guaranteed to improve your game. 144 pages, $12.95.

TOURNAMENT TIPS FROM THE POKER PROS by Shane Smith. Essential advice from poker theorists, authors, and tournament winners on the best strategies for winning the big prizes at low-limit rebuy tournaments. Learn proven strategies for each of the four stages of play—opening, middle, late and final—how to avoid 26 potential traps, advice on rebuys, aggressive play, clock-watching, inside moves, top 20 tips for winning tournaments, more. Advice from Brunson, McEvoy, Cloutier, Caro, Malmuth, others. 160 pages, $14.95.

NO-LIMIT TEXAS HOLD 'EM: The New Player's Guide to Winning Poker's Biggest Game by Brad Daugherty & Tom McEvoy. For experienced limit players who want to play no-limit or rookies who has never played before, two world champions show readers how to evaluate the strength of a hand, determine the amount to bet, understand opponents' play, plus how to bluff and when to do it. Seventy-four game scenarios, unique betting charts for tournament play, and sections on essential principles and strategies show you how to get to the winners circle. Special section on beating online tournaments. 288 pages, $24.95.

GREAT CARDOZA POKER BOOKS
ADD THESE TO YOUR LIBRARY - ORDER NOW!

HOW TO WIN AT OMAHA HIGH-LOW POKER *by Mike Cappelletti*. Clearly written strategies and powerful advice shows the essential winning strategies for beating Omaha high-low poker! This money-making guide includes more than sixty hard-hitting sections on Omaha. Players learn the rules of play, best starting hands, strategies for the flop, turn, and river, how to read the board for both high and low, dangerous draws, and how to beat low-limit tournaments. Includes odds charts, glossary and low-limit tips. 304 pgs, $19.95.

THE BIG BOOK OF POKER *by Ken Warren*. This easy-to-read and oversized guide teaches you everything you need to know to win money at home poker, in cardrooms, casinos, and on the tournament circuit. Readers will learn how to bet, raise, and checkraise, bluff, semi-bluff, and how to take advantage of position and pot odds. Great sections on hold'em (plus stud games, Omaha, draw games, and many more) and playing and winning poker on the internet. Packed with charts, diagrams, sidebars, and detailed, easy-to-read examples by best-selling poker expert Ken Warren, this wonderfully formatted book is one stop shopping for players ready to take on any form of poker for real money. Want to be a big player? Buy the Big Book of Poker! 320 oversized pages, $19.95.

WINNER'S GUIDE TO TEXAS HOLD' EM POKER *by Ken Warren*. New edition shows how to play every hand from every position with every type of flop. Learn the 14 categories of starting hands, the 10 most common hold'em tells, how to evaluate a game for profit, the value of deception, the art of bluffing, eight secrets to winning, starting hand categories, position, and more! Includes detailed analysis of the top 40 hands and the most complete chapter on hold'em odds in print. Over 500,000 copies sold! 224 pages, $14.95.

KEN WARREN TEACHES TEXAS HOLD 'EM *by Ken Warren*. This is a step-by-step comprehensive manual for making money at hold'em poker. 42 powerful chapters teach you one lesson at a time. Great practical advice and concepts with examples from actual games and how to apply them to your own play. Lessons include: Starting Cards, Playing Position, Raising, Check-raising, Tells, Game/Seat Selection, Dominated Hands, Odds, and much more. This book is already a huge fan favorite and best-seller! 416 pages, $26.95.

WINNER'S GUIDE TO OMAHA POKER *by Ken Warren*. Concise and easy-to-understand, Warren shows beginning and intermediate Omaha players how to win from the first time they play. You'll learn the rules, betting and blind structure, why you should play Omaha, the advantages of Omaha over Texas hold'em, glossary, reading the board, basic strategies, Omaha high, Omaha hi-low split 8/better, how to play draws and made hands, evaluation of starting hands, counting outs, computing pot odds, the unique characteristics of split-pot games, the best and worst Omaha hands, how to play before the flop, how to play on the flop, how to play on the turn and river, and much more. 224 pages, $19.95

CHAMPIONSHIP TOURNAMENT POKER *by Tom McEvoy*. Enthusiastically endorsed by more than five world champions, this is a *must* for every player's library. McEvoy lets you in on the secrets he has used to win millions of dollars in tournaments and the insights he has learned competing against the best players in the world. Packed solid with winning strategies for 11 games with extensive discussions of 7-card stud, limit hold'em, pot and no-limit hold'em, Omaha high-low, re-buy, half-half tournaments, satellites, and includes strategies for each stage of tournaments. 416 pages, $29.95.

HOW TO WIN NO-LIMIT HOLD'EM TOURNAMENTS *by McEvoy & Don Vines*. Learn the basic concepts of tournament strategy and how to win big by playing small buy-in events, graduate to medium and big buy-in tournaments, adjust for short fields, huge fields, slow and fast-action events. Plus, how to win online tournaments. You'll also learn how to manage a tournament bankroll and get tips on table demeanor for televised tournaments. See actual hands played by finalists at WSOP and WPT championship tables with card pictures, analysis and useful lessons from the play. 376 pages, $29.95.

GREAT CARDOZA POKER BOOKS
ADD THESE TO YOUR LIBRARY - ORDER NOW!

HOLD'EM WISDOM FOR ALL PLAYERS *By Daniel Negreanu.* Superstar poker player Daniel Negreanu provides 50 easy-to-read and right-to-the-point hold'em strategy nuggets that will immediately make you a better player at cash games and tournaments. His wit and wisdom makes for great reading; even better, it makes for killer winning advice. Conversational, straightforward, and educational, this book covers topics as diverse as the top 10 rookie mistakes to bullying bullies and exploiting your table image. 176 pages, $14.95.

MILLION DOLLAR HOLD'EM: Winning Big in Limit Cash Games by *Johnny Chan and Mark Karowe.* Learn how to win money consistently at limit hold'em, poker's most popular cash game, from one of poker's living legends. You'll get a rare opportunity to get into the mind of the man who has won ten World Series of Poker titles—tied for the most ever with Doyle Brunson—as Johnny picks out illustrative hands and shows how he thinks his way through the betting and the bluffing. No book so thoroughly details the thought process of how a hand is played, the alternative ways it could have been played, and the best way to win session after session. *Essential* reading for cash players. 400 pages, $29.95.

THE POKER TOURNAMENT FORMULA by *Arnold Snyder.* Start making money now in fast no-limit hold'em tournaments with these radical and never-before-published concepts and secrets for beating tournaments. You'll learn why cards don't matter as much as the dynamics of a tournament—your position, the size of your chip stack, who your opponents are, and above all, the structure. Poker tournaments offer one of the richest opportunities to come along in decades. Every so often, a book comes along that changes the way players attack a game and provides them with a big advantage over opponents. Gambling legend Arnold Snyder has written such a book. 368 pages, $19.95.

HOW TO BEAT SIT-AND-GO POKER TOURNAMENTS by Neil Timothy. There is a lot of dead money up for grabs in the lower limit sit-and-gos and Neil Timothy shows you how to go and get it. The author, a professional player, shows you how to reach the last six places of lower limit sit-and-go tournaments four out of five times and then how to get in the money 25-35 percent of the time using his powerful, proven strategies. This book can turn a losing sit-and-go player into a winner, and a winner into a bigger winner. Also effective for the early and middle stages of one-table satellites. 176 pages, $14.95.

HOW TO BEAT INTERNET CASINOS AND POKER ROOMS by *Arnold Snyder.* Learn how to play and win money online against the Internet casinos. Snyder shows you how to choose safe sites to play. He goes over every step of the process, from choosing sites and opening an account to how to take your winnings home! Snyder covers the differences between "brick and mortar" and Internet gaming rooms and how to handle common situations and predicaments. A major chapter covers Internet poker and basic strategies to beat hold'em and other games online. 272 pages, $14.95..

I'M ALL IN: High Stakes, Big Business, and the Birth of the World Poker *Tour* by *Lyle Berman with Marvin Karlins.* Lyle Berman recounts how he revolutionized and revived the game of poker and transformed America's culture in the process. Get the inside story of the man who created the World Poker Tour, plus the exciting world of high-stakes gambling where a million dollars can be won or lost in a single game. Lyle reveals the 13 secrets of being a successful businessman, how poker players self-destruct, the 7 essential principles of winning at poker. Foreword by Donald Trump. Hardback, photos. 232 pages, $24.95.

7-CARD STUD: The Complete Course in Winning at Medium & Lower Limits by *Roy West.* Learn the latest strategies for winning at $1-$4 spread-limit up to $10/$20 fixed-limit games. Covers starting hands, 3rd-7th street strategy, overcards, selective aggressiveness, reading hands, pro secrets, psychology, and more in an informal 42 lesson format. Includes bonus chapter on 7-stud tournament strategy by Tom McEvoy. 224 pages, $19.95.

DOYLE BRUNSON'S EXCITING BOOKS
ADD THESE TO YOUR COLLECTION - ORDER NOW!

SUPER SYSTEM by *Doyle Brunson*. This classic book is considered by the pros to be the best book ever written on poker! Jam-packed with advanced strategies, theories, tactics and money-making techniques, no serious poker player can afford to be without this hard-hitting information. Includes fifty pages of the most precise poker statistics ever published. Features chapters written by poker's biggest superstars, such as Dave Sklansky, Mike Caro, Chip Reese, Joey Hawthorne, Bobby Baldwin, and Doyle. Essential strategies, advanced play, and no-nonsense winning advice on making money at 7-card stud (razz, high-low split, cards speak, and declare), draw poker, lowball, and hold'em (limit and no-limit).This is a must-read for any serious poker player. 628 pages, $29.95.

SUPER SYSTEM 2 by *Doyle Brunson*. The most anticipated poker book ever, SS2 expands upon the original with more games and professional secrets from the best in the world. Superstar contributors include Daniel Negreanu, winner of multiple WSOP gold bracelets and 2004 Poker Player of the Year; Lyle Berman, 3-time WSOP gold bracelet winner, founder of the World Poker Tour, and super-high stakes cash player; Bobby Baldwin, 1978 World Champion; Johnny Chan, 2-time World Champion and 10-time WSOP bracelet winner; Mike Caro, poker's greatest researcher, theorist, and instructor; Jennifer Harman, the world's top female player and one of ten best overall; Todd Brunson, winner of more than 20 tournaments; and Crandell Addington, no-limit hold'em legend. 672 pgs, $34.95.

CARO'S GUIDE TO DOYLE BRUNSON'S SUPER SYSTEM by *Mike Caro*. Working with World Champion Doyle Brunson, the legendary Mike Caro has created a fresh look to the "Bible" of all poker books, adding new and personal insights that help you understand the original work. Caro breaks 36 concepts into either "Analysis, Commentary, Concept, Mission, Play-By-Play, Psychology, Statistics, Story, or Strategy. Lots of illustrations and winning concepts give even more value to this great work. 86 pages, 8 1/2 x 11, $19.95.

ACCORDING TO DOYLE by *Doyle Brunson*. Learn what it takes to be a great poker player by climbing inside the mind of poker's most famous champion. Fascinating anecdotes and adventures from Doyle's early career playing poker in roadhouses are interspersed with lessons from the champion who has made more money at poker than anyone else in history. Learn what makes a great player tick, how he approaches the game, and receive candid, powerful advice from the legend himself. 208 pages, $14.95.

MY 50 MOST MEMORABLE HANDS by *Doyle Brunson*. This instant classic relives the most incredible hands by the greatest poker player of all time. Great players, legends, and poker's most momentous events march in and out of fifty years of unforgettable hands. Sit side-by-side with Doyle as he replays the excitement and life-changing moments of the most thrilling and crucial hands in the history of poker: from his early games as a rounder in the rough-and-tumble "Wild West" years—where a man was more likely to get shot as he was to get a straight flush—to the nail-biting excitement of his two world championship titles. Relive million dollar hands and the high stakes tension of sidestepping police, hijackers and murderers. A thrilling collection of stories and sage poker advice. 168 pages, $14.95.

ONLINE POKER by *Doyle Brunson*. Ten compelling chapters show you how to get started, explain the safety features which lets you play worry-free, and lets you in on the strategies that Doyle himself uses to beat players in cyberspace. Poker is poker, as Doyle explains, but there are also strategies that only apply to the online version, where the players are weaker!—and Doyle reveals them all in this book.192 pages, illustrations, $14.95.

BOBBY BALDWIN'S WINNING POKER SECRETS by *Mike Caro with Bobby Baldwin*. The fascinating account of 1978 World Champion Bobby Baldwin's early career playing poker against other legends is packed with valuable insights. Covers the common mistakes average players make at seven poker variations and the dynamic winning concepts needed for success. Endorsed by superstars Doyle Brunson and Amarillo Slim. 208 pages, $14.95.

MIKE CARO'S EXCITING WORK
POWERFUL BOOKS YOU **MUST** HAVE

CARO'S MOST PROFITABLE HOLD'EM ADVICE *by Mike Caro.* When Mike Caro writes a book on winning, all poker players take notice. And they should: The "Mad Genius of Poker" has influenced just about every professional player and world champion alive. You'll journey far beyond the traditional tactical tools offered in most poker books and for the first time, have access to the entire missing arsenal of strategies left out of everything you've ever seen or experienced. Caro's first major work in two decades is packed with hundreds of powerful ideas, concepts, and strategies, many of which will be new to you—they have never been made available to the general public. This book represents Caro's lifelong research into beating the game of hold em. 408 pages, $24.95

MASTERING HOLD'EM AND OMAHA *by Mike Caro and Mike Cappelletti.* Learn the professional secrets to mastering the two most popular games of big-money poker: hold'em and Omaha. This is a thinking player's book, packed with ideas, with the focus is on making you a winning player. You'll learn everything from the strategies for play on the preflop, flop, turn and river, to image control and taking advantage of players stuck in losing patterns. You'll also learn how to create consistent winning patterns, use perception to gain an edge, avoid common errors, go after and win default pots, recognize and use the various types of raises, play marginal hands for profit, the importance of being loved or feared, and Cappelletti's unique point count system for Omaha. 328 pages, $19.95.

CARO'S BOOK OF POKER TELLS *by Mike Caro.* One of the ten greatest books written on poker, this must-have book should be in every player's library. If you're serious about winning, you'll realize that most of the profit comes from being able to read your opponents. Caro reveals the the secrets of interpreting *tells*—physical reactions that reveal information about a player's cards—such as shrugs, sighs, shaky hands, eye contact, and many more. Learn when opponents are bluffing, when they aren't and why—based solely on their mannerisms. Over 170 photos of players in action and play-by-play examples show the actual tells. These powerful ideas will give you the decisive edge. 320 pages, $24.95.

CARO'S FUNDAMENTAL SECRETS OF WINNING POKER *by Mike Caro.* Learn the essential strategies, concepts, and plays that comprise the very foundation of winning poker play. Learn to win more from weak players, equalize stronger players, bluff a bluffer, win big pots, where to sit against weak players, and the six factors of strategic table image. Includes selected tips on hold 'em, 7 stud, draw, lowball, tournaments, more. 160 pages, $12.95.

CARO'S PROFESSIONAL POKER REPORTS

Each of these three powerful insider poker reports is centered around a daily mission, with the goal of adding one weapon per day to your arsenal. Theoretical concepts and practical situations are mixed together for fast in-depth learning. For serious players.

11 DAYS TO 7-STUD SUCCESS. Bluffing, playing and defending pairs, different strategies for the different streets, analyzing situations—lots of information within. One advantage is gained each day. A quick and powerful method to 7-stud winnings. Essential. Signed, numbered. $19.95.

12 DAYS TO HOLD'EM SUCCESS. Positional thinking, playing and defending against mistakes, small pairs, flop situations, playing the river, are just some sample lessons. Guaranteed to make you a better player. Very popular. Signed, numbered. $19.95.

PROFESSIONAL 7-STUD REPORT. When to call, pass, and raise, playing starting hands, aggressive play, 4th and 5th street concepts, lots more. Tells how to read an opponent's starting hand, plus sophisticated advanced strategies. Important revision for serious players. Signed, numbered. $19.95.

THE CHAMPIONSHIP SERIES
POWERFUL INFORMATION YOU <u>MUST</u> HAVE

CHAMPIONSHIP NO-LIMIT & POT-LIMIT HOLD'EM *by T. J. Cloutier & Tom McEvoy.* The bible for winning pot-limit and no-limit hold'em tournaments gives you all the answers to your most important questions: How do you get inside your opponents' heads and learn how to beat them at their own game? How can you tell how much to bet, raise, and reraise in no-limit hold'em? When can you bluff? How do you set up your opponents in pot-limit hold'em so that you can win a monster pot? What are the best strategies for winning no-limit and pot-limit tournaments, satellites, and supersatellites? Rock-solid and inspired advice you can bank on from two of the most recognizable figures in poker. 304 pages, $29.95.

CHAMPIONSHIP HOLD'EM *by T. J. Cloutier & Tom McEvoy.* Hard-hitting hold'em the way it's played *today* in both limit cash games and tournaments. Get killer advice on how to win more money in rammin'-jammin' games, kill-pot, jackpot, shorthanded, and full table cash games. You'll learn the thinking process for preflop, flop, turn, and river play with specific suggestions for what to do when good or bad things happen. Includes play-by-play analyses, advice on how to maximize profits against rocks in tight games, weaklings in loose games, experts in solid games, plus tournament strategies for small buy-in, big buy-in, rebuy, add-on, satellite and big-field major tournaments. Wow! 392 pages, $29.95.

CHAMPIONSHIP OMAHA (Omaha High-Low, Pot-limit Omaha, Limit High Omaha) *by Tom McEvoy & T.J. Cloutier.* Clearly-written strategies and powerful advice from Cloutier and McEvoy who have won four World Series of Poker Omaha titles. You'll learn how to beat low-limit and high-stakes games, play against loose and tight opponents, and the differing strategies for rebuy and freezeout tournaments. Learn the best starting hands, when slowplaying a big hand is dangerous, what danglers are (and why winners don't play them), why you sometimes fold the nuts on the flop and would be correct in doing so, and overall, how you can win a lot of money at Omaha! 296 pages, illustrations, $29.95.

CHAMPIONSHIP HOLD'EM TOURNAMENT HANDS *by T. J. Cloutier & Tom McEvoy.* An absolute must for hold'em tournament players, two legends show you how to become a winning tournament player at both limit and no-limit hold'em games. Get inside the authors' heads as they think their way through the correct strategy at 57 limit and no-limit starting hands. Cloutier & McEvoy show you how to use skill and intuition to play strategic hands for maximum profit in real tournament scenarios and how 45 key hands were played by champions in turnaround situations at the WSOP. Gain tremendous insights into how tournament poker is played at the highest levels. 368 pages, $29.95.

CHAMPIONSHIP HOLD'EM SATELLITE STRATEGY *by World Champions Brad Dougherty & Tom McEvoy.* Every year satellite players win their way into the $10,000 WSOP buy-in and emerge as millionaires or champions. You can too! Learn the specific, proven strategies for winning almost any satellite from two world champions. Covers the ten ways to win a seat at the WSOP, how to win limit hold'em and no-limit hold'em satellites, one-table satellites, online satellites, and the final table of super satellites. Includes a special chapter on no-limit hold'em satellites! 320 pages, $29.95.

HOW TO WIN THE CHAMPIONSHIP: Hold'em Strategies for the Final Table, *by T.J. Cloutier.* If you're hungry to win a championship, this is the book that will pave the way! T.J. Cloutier, the greatest tournament poker player ever—he has won 60 major tournament titles and appeared at 39 final tables at the WSOP, both more than any other player in the history of poker—shows how to get to the final table where the big money is made and then how to win it all. You'll learn how to build up enough chips to make it through the early and middle rounds and then how to employ T.J.'s own strategies to outmaneuver opponents at the final table and win championships. You'll learn how to adjust your play depending upon stack sizes, antes/blinds, table position, opponents styles, chip counts, and the specific strategies for six-handed, three handed, and heads-up play. 288 pages, $29.95.

POWERFUL WINNING POKER SIMULATIONS
A MUST FOR SERIOUS PLAYERS WITH A COMPUTER!
IBM compatible CD ROM Win 95, 98, 2000, NT, ME, XP

These incredible full color poker simulations are the best method to improve your game. Computer opponents play like real players. All games let you set the limits and rake and have fully programmable players, plus stat tracking, and Hand Analyzer for starting hands. Mike Caro, the world's foremost poker theoretician says, "Amazing... a steal for under $500... get it, it's great." Includes free phone support. "Smart Advisor" gives expert advice for every play!

NEW!
Windows Versions
More Features!

1. TURBO TEXAS HOLD'EM FOR WINDOWS - $59.95. Choose which players, and how many (2-10) you want to play, create loose/tight games, and control check-raising, bluffing, position, sensitivity to pot odds, and more! Also, instant replay, pop-up odds, Professional Advisor keeps track of play statistics. Free bonus: Hold'em Hand Analyzer analyzes all 169 pocket hands in detail and their win rates under any conditions you set. Caro says this "hold'em software is the most powerful ever created." Great product!

2. TURBO SEVEN-CARD STUD FOR WINDOWS - $59.95. Create any conditions of play; choose number of players (2-8), bet amounts, fixed or spread limit, bring-in method, tight/loose conditions, position, reaction to board, number of dead cards, and stack deck to create special conditions. Features instant replay. Terrific stat reporting includes analysis of starting cards, 3-D bar charts, and graphs. Play interactively and run high speed simulation to test strategies. Hand Analyzer analyzes starting hands in detail. Wow!

3. TURBO OMAHA HIGH-LOW SPLIT FOR WINDOWS - $59.95. Specify any playing conditions; betting limits, number of raises, blind structures, button position, aggressiveness/passiveness of opponents, number of players (2-10), types of hands dealt, blinds, position, board reaction, and specify flop, turn, and river cards! Choose opponents and use provided point count or create your own. Statistical reporting, instant replay, pop-up odds high speed simulation to test strategies, amazing Hand Analyzer, and much more!

4. TURBO OMAHA HIGH FOR WINDOWS - $59.95. Same features as above, but tailored for Omaha High only. Caro says program is "an electrifying research tool...it can clearly be worth thousands of dollars to any serious player. A must for Omaha High players.

5. TURBO 7 STUD 8 OR BETTER - $59.95. Brand new with all the features you expect from the Wilson Turbo products: the latest artificial intelligence, instant advice and exact odds, play versus 2-7 opponents, enhanced data charts that can be exported or printed, the ability to fold out of turn and immediately go to the next hand, ability to peek at opponents hand, optional warning mode that warns you if a play disagrees with the advisor, and automatic mode that runs up to 50 tests unattended. Tough computer players vary their styles for a great game.

---

6. TOURNAMENT TEXAS HOLD'EM - $39.95

Set-up for tournament practice and play, this realistic simulation pits you against celebrity look-alikes. Tons of options let you control tournament size with 10 to 300 entrants, select limits, ante, rake, blind structures, freezeouts, number of rebuys and competition level of opponents. Pop-up status report shows how you're doing vs. the competition. Save tournaments in progress to play again later. Additional feature allows quick folds on finished hands.

255